Homegrown Violent Extremism

Homegrown Violent Extremism

Erroll Southers

ELSEVIER

AMSTERDAM • BOSTON • HEIDELBERG • LONDON
NEW YORK • OXFORD • PARIS • SAN DIEGO
SAN FRANCISCO • SINGAPORE • SYDNEY • TOKYO
Anderson Publishing is an imprint of Elsevier

Anderson Publishing is an imprint of Elsevier
The Boulevard, Langford Lane, Kidlington, Oxford, OX5 1GB, UK
225 Wyman Street, Waltham, MA 02451, USA

First published 2013

Notices
Knowledge and best practice in this field are constantly changing. As new research and experience broaden our understanding, changes in research methods, professional practices, or medical treatment may become necessary.

Practitioners and researchers must always rely on their own experience and knowledge in evaluating and using any information, methods, compounds, or experiments described herein. In using such information or methods they should be mindful of their own safety and the safety of others, including parties for whom they have a professional responsibility.

To the fullest extent of the law, neither the Publisher nor the authors, contributors, or editors, assume any liability for any injury and/or damage to persons or property as a matter of products liability, negligence or otherwise, or from any use or operation of any methods, products, instructions, or ideas contained in the material herein.

British Library Cataloguing-in-Publication Data
A catalogue record for this book is available from the British Library

Library of Congress Cataloging-in-Publication Data
A catalog record for this book is available from the Library of Congress

ISBN: 978-1-4557-7643-6

For information on all Anderson publications
visit our website at **store.elsevier.com**

This book has been manufactured using Print On Demand technology. Each copy is produced to order and is limited to black ink. The online version of this book will show color figures where appropriate.

Working together
to grow libraries in
developing countries

www.elsevier.com • www.bookaid.org

Transferred to Digital Printing in 2013

CONTENTS

ACKNOWLEDGMENTS

This book comes on the heels of several years of focused research and study, as well as a counterterrorism and law enforcement career that spans more than three decades. As such, I have a lifetime of people to thank.

First, I must thank Elsevier for their support and readiness to publish on this important topic and Ehsan Zeffar for the introduction. I also owe a great deal of thanks and appreciation to Dr. Eric Heikkila, my doctoral committee chair. His tireless support, guidance and encouragement helped make this book come to fruition. Thanks also to the members of my doctoral committee—Boaz Ganor, Michael Orosz, Peter Robertson and Milind Tambe—all experts in their respective disciplines who provided invaluable expertise and insight.

This work would not have been possible without the support of the University of Southern California and my Trojan Family; the Sol Price School of Public Policy, Viterbi School of Engineering, and the National Center for Risk and Economic Analysis for Terrorism Events (CREATE). I also offer a special thanks to President Max Nikias, Deans Jack Knott and Yannis Yortsos, Vice Dean Elizabeth Graddy, Associate Dean Regina Nordahl, Catie Burke, Director Stephen Hora, Deborah Natoli, Isaac Maya, Martin Krieger, Dan Haverty, Kelly Buccola, Erin Callichio, Carmen Gomez, Stan Henderson, Sabrina Feeley, and Heather Rosoff.

I also owe a great deal to my very dear mentors and incredible friends: Arnold Schwarzenegger, Rep. Jane Harman, Rep. Bennie Thompson, Secretary Janet Napolitano, Bonnie Reiss, Peter Bergen, Frank Quiambao, Brian Keith, Matthew Bettenhausen, Connie Rice, Claire Vasios, Randy Parsons, Don Leighton, Jim Butts, Jim Featherstone, Arif Alikhan, Brian Banning, Rich Callahan, Jim Davis, Amy Zegart, Ron Iden, Bill Leider, Ivan Newman, Maria Ressa, Fran Townsend, Richard Clarke, Hon. Michael Chertoff, Joanne St. Lewis, Daveed Gartenstein-Ross, Alexandra Lieben, Fred Roberts, Johnathan Tal, Edan Gottlib, Doron Pely, Larry Dietz, Peter Franklin, Julie

Cruzal, Elliot Brandt, my colleagues at the Interdisciplinary Center in Herzliya, Israel and my attorneys, Marc Cohen and Sheri Jeffrey. The editorial guidance of my writing partner, Justin Hienz, is extraordinary. His knowledge and organization helped get this work completed ahead of schedule. Perhaps most important among these, my dear friend Desmond Saunders-Newton, who passed before this work was completed. I know he would be proud that I heeded his advice.

This work represents another important step in the collective national effort to protect the United States. I thank the academics, practitioners and other experts who have developed our counterterrorism capabilities to what they are today, and I respectfully stand on their shoulders to continue this important effort.

None of this would have been possible without the unconditional support and extraordinary patience of my mom and dad, my children, my brother David, an incredible writer in his own right, and my wife Caryn. I owe more to her than any book acknowledgement can express. She will finally be able to make a meal without my interruptions to read or listen to countless drafts.

And thank you, reader, for taking the time and interest to read this humble contribution to the ongoing international discussion about security and methods for preventing violent extremism. People fear what they don't understand.

Since September 11, 2001, security experts, law enforcement professionals and government leaders have been expecting another terrorist attack. Even as the United States and other countries have vastly improved their security posture through billions of dollars in technology and operational investments, training, and policy improvements, there has been a solemn recognition that no matter how advanced and coordinated a country's security efforts, eventually, a terrorist would find vulnerability in the system and exploit it.

On April 15, 2013, in Boston, the inevitable occurred. Two men—Tamerlan and Dzhokhar Tsarnaev—placed pressure cooker bombs amid the crowd gathered at the finish line of the Boston Marathon. Spectator cameras were recording when these bombs exploded, sending fireballs into the air and hurling shrapnel into the hundreds of people nearby. The blasts killed three people and injured 264 others. It was the first successful attack on U.S. soil since 9/11, and it was the first attack on a sporting event since the 1996 Olympic Games.

While an attack of some form had been expected for years, the big questions for security professionals were always where, when and from whom would an attack come? Osama bin Laden and al Qaeda dominated the public gaze for nearly a decade. The wars in Afghanistan and Iraq, as well as joint operations in Yemen, Pakistan, Saudi Arabia and other countries, focused the military response to transnational terrorism squarely on the al Qaeda threat. This severely disrupted the primary organization and its satellites (such as al Qaeda in the Arabian Peninsula). Funding was cut off, leaders were killed and communications were intercepted. While there remains some vestige of the terrorist organization, it is a shell of what it was on 9/11. The United States, with the help of its allies, put an end to core al Qaeda. But we did not end terrorism. That is, tragically, impossible.

There is limited capacity and opportunity for international terrorists to plot and launch attacks against the United States from abroad. Aviation and immigration security, far-reaching intelligence gathering, and an increasingly aware and alert public make another 9/11-style attack a remote possibility. While violent extremists operating in lawless, poverty-stricken, failing states have little chance of planning and executing a major terrorist attack, the United States and other countries have always feared another kind of threat—one that is vastly more difficult to anticipate and interrupt. As seen in Boston, when terrorism arises from within a domestic population, there is often little warning. Once homegrown adversaries are in motion, it is incredibly difficult to detect and stop them.

Within the context of America, this homegrown violent extremism (HVE) is terrorist activity or plots targeting the United States and U.S. assets by American citizens or residents who have embraced their extremist ideology largely within this country. This threat is diverse and growing.

As a basis for any thoughtful analysis of HVE, it must be accepted that total security—that is, the permanent absence of a terrorist threat—is unobtainable. No matter how effective the security technology or refined the processes, we as a society can never be fully free of the threat from violent extremism. There are, however, ways to reduce risk and improve our counterterrorism efforts. This necessitates a robust understanding of HVE and radicalization, which is the purpose of this book.

I.1 OVERCOMING THE "OTHER" MINDSET

Any terrorist attack causes a predictable level of chaos and uncertainty. Immediately after the Boston bombing, law enforcement, the FBI and other intelligence organizations shifted into high gear. The Boston police department communications center dispatched a constant stream of reports about suspicious packages and unknown individuals. Every potential unattended bag or unidentified person became suspect, and for hours after the attack, police rushed from one location to another, assuming out of necessity that there were more bombs waiting to explode. Thankfully, there were not.

Within hours of the attack, law enforcement identified a "Saudi national" who had been at the marathon as a person of interest. This man had been wounded by shrapnel, and he was kept under armed guard at the hospital. Ultimately, we learned that he was just one of the hundreds of bombing victims. Yet, that he became a person of interest to begin with shows where suspicion fell before all the facts were available. We were looking for foreigners.

This reveals a critical flaw in our collective understanding of terrorism, a misplaced belief that evildoers necessarily only come from other countries. They must look different, practice a different faith, and hold a different nationality. They are "other" than us. Yet, the attack in Boston showed this to be a miscalculation. The origin of the ideology is irrelevant in determining homegrown versus international terrorism; what matters is where it is embraced.

After several days, the Tsarnaev brothers were identified as the attackers, and the ensuing manhunt ended with a dramatic shootout and standoff. While the brothers were born in another country, they had been living in the United States for more than a decade. Both men grew up in the United States, without any overt indications that they would someday choose a life of terrorism. The older brother, Tamerlan, was a legal U.S. resident who had found some difficulty attaining citizenship. The younger brother, Dzhokhar, however, was an American, having taken the oath of citizenship, ironically, on September 11, 2012.

It is believed these men traversed a process of self-radicalization in the United States, perhaps enhanced by skills gained during Tamerlan's overseas trip just months before the attack. Regardless, the brothers were locals, educated, living and working in the area. The Tsarnaevs walked into infamy alone and within U.S. borders, making them, by definition, homegrown violent extremists.

The terrorist threat to the United States is not as neat and clearly defined as we would like. If the terrorists of the world all looked the same, followed the same ideology and used the same tactics, America might be able to achieve total security. An infallible security system and a uniform terrorist threat, however, do not exist. There is no single group on which we can focus our counterterrorism efforts. There is no easy way to know in advance who among us will lead a peaceful existence and who will endeavor to cause mass death, destruction, and fear. Terrorism messaging has benefited significantly from globalization. Ideas that might seem distant and foreign are also right here, at home. Likewise, the ideologies that grow in the United States also reach around the world. Whenever we attempt to fit the terrorist threat into clear-cut borders and definitions, we fail to anticipate the whole threat, which has no common nationality, motivation, or profile.

To address the broader challenge of preventing terrorist attacks that originate with citizens and residents (rather than foreign adversaries), we must take on a more nuanced, thoughtful and intelligent perspective of HVE, its origins, and the methods for interrupting those on a pathway to violence. Part of this strategy includes focused efforts to counter the extremist ideologies and messages that propel individuals through the radicalization process.

I.2 UNDERSTANDING THE RADICALIZATION PATHWAY

As the world learned, the Tsarnaev brothers were motivated by an extremist Muslim Identity ideology. For many, this seemed to be an indication that irrespective of nationality, the terrorist threat is predominantly driven by an extremist interpretation of Islamic beliefs. To be sure, there are myriad examples of terrorists who fall within this camp, but maintaining a limited focus on Muslim Identity creates a profound blind spot in our national security efforts.

Since the start of the Obama Administration, there has been an unprecedented increase in domestic extremist groups. The election of an African-American president with an Arabic sounding name and a Muslim father, as well as public debate over his place of birth, fueled anti-government sentiment and extremist ideologies. This has swelled the ranks of groups that view the federal government as the enemy, feeding ideologies that see the government as an illegitimate corporation of elites planning to implement a "one-world government." While the terrorist threat these groups pose has not received broad coverage in mainstream media reporting, their thwarted plots include the intended bombing of federal buildings, assassination of public officials, attacks on uniformed law enforcement and the use of biological agents against the public.

For many, violent extremism has become synonymous with Islamic radicalism, but this is a woefully myopic view. Religious belief is only one example of legitimizing ideology that can contribute to violent activity. Ultimately, it is not the ideology itself that propels HVE; it is a combination of many factors that together create conditions under which someone might cross the line from extremist rhetoric to violent action. This is the radicalization pathway.

HVE radicalization is not a conveyor belt that starts with a set of grievances and ends with violence, with easily discernible signposts along the way. It is a path through a complex and changing social and psychological landscape that is unique to every individual. What causes one person to embrace violent extremism may not have the same effect on another. There is no HVE checklist that can be used to identify someone in the midst of the radicalization process and determine whether they will turn violent.

In the investigation into the Boston bombing, authorities have focused on Tamerlan Tsarnaev's 6-month trip to Chechnya, which preceded the attack. Whatever he did there and whomever he met with likely contributed to Tsarnaev's plans, but we can be reasonably assured that his path to HVE began long before his trip to his family's motherland. Like other violent extremists, Tsarnaev's radicalization was a long progression of experiences and grievances, nearly all of which occurred within the United States.

The radicalization process often begins with a "cognitive opening," an event or experience that yields a personal grievance, which in turn makes someone more susceptible to accepting an extremist ideology. Grievances take many forms, such as conflicted identities, injustice, oppression or socioeconomic exclusion. Critically, there is no way of knowing what an individual will internalize as a life-changing grievance. What is devastating to one person may be irrelevant to another.

Even as grievance may lead to a broader openness to an ideology, it is not simply the belief in extremist ideologies that leads to HVE. There are many people who hold extremist views but do not engage in violent activity. While understanding how grievances can feed into an ideology is one avenue for addressing the potential for violent extremism, the radicalization pathway is not limited to any one racial, religious or issue-oriented group. It is a crosscutting phenomenon with an ever-uncertain end. It is often impossible to know who will exit the radicalization pathway as a violent extremist until they do so.

It is important to note the role online media can play in fostering violent extremism. Arguably, the Internet's capacity for propelling extremists through the radicalization process is the single most important and dangerous innovation to the terrorist threat since the 9/11 attacks. Future attacks against the United States and its interests will likely involve adversaries who have traversed the radicalization process, at least in part, online.

In searching for a comprehensive understanding of violent extremism and those engaged in the radicalization process, history teaches valuable lessons, if we are willing to learn. After the bombing of Pearl Harbor, the United States declared martial law and interned 110,000 Japanese Americans. More than two-thirds of those interned were American citizens, and half of them were children. In some cases, family members were separated and sent to different camps. None had ever shown disloyalty to the nation, and throughout the war, none of the people convicted of spying for Japan were of Japanese or Asian ancestry. The internment was a monumental policy failure on a number of levels. The lesson with regard to HVE is that attempts to identify and disrupt threats must be evidence-based. Often, targeting potential adversaries according to one broad category (such as ethnicity or religion) leads to unjust scrutiny of innocent individuals.

Terrorism requires a combination of three things: an alienated individual, a legitimizing ideology (engaged through radicalization) and an enabling environment. Of the three, it is the environment that is most susceptible to positive influences. While it is tempting to focus counterterrorism efforts on alienated, extremist individuals, recognizing that the goal is to contain terrorism and not simply stop terrorists, we must support and collaborate with communities to identify people on the path to violent extremism. Indeed, working with communities, we have the potential to disrupt the radicalization pathway altogether.

I.3 FOSTERING COMMUNITY ENGAGEMENT

Our best chance for preventing terrorist incidents is to embrace a more holistic, community-based effort. Counterterrorism and law enforcement professionals have limited resources. Given the plethora of threats to a safe society, as well as the foggy, often-unseen radicalization process that can take place anywhere, anytime, those with the greatest capacity to identify and help disrupt the path to violent extremism are the very communities from which potential terrorists arise.

Every terrorist has a family, a network of friends and acquaintances, and a local environment where they live and work. Knowing that the path to violent extremism is long and complex, it is essential that those charged with preventing terrorism work with communities to implement programs and foster transparency and information sharing. This can help identify individuals who are susceptible to turning violent—but critically, *before* they do so.

This community-based effort should help policy makers and community members identify challenges and develop collaborative strategies to improve the community's general wellbeing. The community-based effort is not focused solely on reducing the risk of HVE, nor is it driven by law enforcement. Unlike traditional community-based policing, which has shown some positive results, this strategy enhances relationship building and information sharing, emphasizing an overall improvement in the community's quality of life.

Public awareness and engagement is an effective supplement to the dedicated work of America's security, intelligence and law enforcement professionals. No one knows an area better than the local community, and no one is more attuned to troubling changes in an individual's beliefs and behavior than those who know them on a personal level. Extremist beliefs are as individual and varied as the people who embrace them. As such, we must build the public vigilance and capacity to identify potentially threatening individuals, creating a mosaic of engagement that supports and amplifies our national security.

Community inaction—either through tacit approval of extremist ideas or a hesitancy to speak up when encountering an individual exploring a legitimizing ideology—provides an enabling environment that allows extremism to fester and sometimes mature into violence. Conversely, engaged and alert community members who are willing to report suspicious activities provide an invaluable resource in the broader national security effort. They can help disrupt the radicalization process, thereby undermining terrorism. This means addressing grievances, as well as recognizing and encouraging stakeholder engagement. We should seek out opportunities to empower communities to this end.

Doing so requires strong bonds between law enforcement, security professionals and the communities they strive to protect. Singling out a person or entire community as suspect based on limited criteria (such as religion alone) undermines the public cohesion that is essential to collective efforts and information sharing. When individuals or communities feel marginalized by profiling, they become increasingly unwilling to share knowledge of potentially violent extremist activity. Additionally, this may create opportunities for extremist groups to recruit individuals who feel victimized by oppressive public policies. Thus, not only is a focus on one legitimizing ideology over another inadequate in terms of assessing and preparing for a range of potential threats, it can also hinder the community collaboration that might disrupt the radicalization process and prevent terrorist activity.

I.4 TOWARD AN ACADEMIC STUDY OF HVE

The information and analysis presented here is intended to build a comprehensive understanding of HVE. Perhaps one of the greatest challenges to a discipline-wide discussion of HVE is a definition of the phenomenon itself. To that end, Chapter 1 introduces the complexities of defining terrorism generally and HVE specifically. Violent extremism as a phenomenon is explored through its multifaceted characteristics, the role of a legitimizing ideology and the factors that contribute to violent action.

With a clearer understanding of precisely what is meant by the term HVE, Chapter 2 investigates the numerous groups that embrace a range of extremist doctrines. Race, religion and issue-oriented ideologies come in many forms, as do the groups that espouse beliefs in line with these ideologies. Looking closely at HVE ideological motivations, missions and long-term objectives helps reveal the central factors that become associated with terrorist acts. As shown, it is clear that ideological adherents can come to embrace a hybrid of beliefs, and some of the most troubling extremist ideologies are followed and spread by non-Muslim Identity groups. These groups employ sophisticated strategies for furthering their extremist beliefs and objectives under the guise of constitutionally-protected activities.

With knowledge of the diverse ideologies followed by different groups throughout the United States, and indeed, the world, Chapter 3 examines the complex components in the radicalization process. As a part of this, the chapter also looks closely at the role of community in the trajectory toward violent extremism. As the community is the one element that may reduce the potential for recruitment and radicalization, contributing factors and challenges are examined with a view toward the development of a community-based, risk-reduction model. Essential elements facilitating the model, such as leadership styles, group behavior research, and associated theoretical structures, illustrate areas where research and policy challenges need to be addressed.

Chapter 4 discusses how counterterrorism should evolve in professional practice. The development of security and counterterrorism tactics has not necessarily yielded a true academic discipline focused on understanding and countering violent extremism. To encourage a more robust field, the chapter examines core questions and research methodologies in the humanities, sciences and social sciences. This helps reveal each discipline's value proposition and how these diverse areas of study may be leveraged into HVE research. The scientific method and critical theory, when applied to the study of extremists and extremist group relationships, provide the capacity to identify appropriate research questions critical to strategies for countering extremist ideologies.

Finally, Chapter 5 introduces the *Mosaic of Engagement* model, a "whole of community" concept designed to improve community quality of life by enhancing public safety generally, while challenging and containing violent extremism specifically. The model examines the achievements and shortcomings of the United Kingdom's Preventing Violent Extremism Strategy, which was considered one of the most innovative counterterrorism programs in the world when it was first implemented. As well as drawing from the best-practice outcomes of the "community indicators" model in City Heights, San Diego, *Mosaic* incorporates lessons learned from both programs to develop a community and school-based model for limiting circumstances and factors that can facilitate HVE recruitment and radicalization.

As shown throughout this book, HVE is hardly a fully defined and exhaustively researched phenomenon. Indeed, academia and the security professions are just beginning to understand this evolving challenge to public safety. The threat requires a risk-based response; there is no comprehensive strategy that yields 100% security. Rather, we are challenged to approach the terrorist threat in a new way, with a more nuanced understanding of how violent extremism originates and erupts.

Notwithstanding the serious threats to national security posed by al Qaeda and its affiliates, we focus *only* on this specific group (and Muslim Identity ideologies) at our great peril. HVE is defining the twenty-first century terrorist threat. The United States and many other countries face creative, adaptive adversaries. Some we have identified; others continue to operate in the shadows.

If the Boston marathon bombing taught us anything about HVE, it is that we cannot hope to thwart terrorist attacks by using only our current models of terrorism. We have an obligation to update our understanding of terrorism and violent extremism such that it accurately reflects the nature of the evolving threat. This book is intended to be a catalyst that will keep our collective efforts moving forward, toward a more effective response to the ever-present threat from HVE.

CHAPTER 1

Defining Homegrown Violent Extremism

Homegrown violent extremism (HVE) represents the next challenge for counterterrorism, but addressing the threat with effective risk-reduction and intelligence-driven security demands a clear understanding of what constitutes HVE. What is "homegrown?" Is HVE synonymous with domestic terrorism?

Much like the word "terrorism," there is no comprehensive definition for HVE. For homegrown and foreign actors alike, there is no consistency with regard to race, religious belief, national origin, ethnicity, gender, sexual orientation or indeed, any other characteristic (aside from the desire to attack structures or people to achieve an ideologically driven societal, governmental, or economic goal).

Recognizing that one size does not fit all in the counterterrorism lexicon, this book uses the following definition as a baseline for comparative analysis of the homegrown phenomenon:

> *HVE describes a terrorist act within the context of ideologically motivated violence or plots, perpetrated within the United States or abroad by American citizens, residents or visitors, who have embraced their legitimizing ideology largely within the United States.*

Within this definition are three primary terms requiring further description. These are a definition of a "terrorist act;"; an examination of what constitutes extremism and violent extremism; and the characteristics of a "homegrown" adversary.

1.1 WHAT IS TERRORISM?

There are few words more emotionally or politically charged than "terrorism." Even before the world entered the post-9/11 era, attempts to define terrorism confounded academics. There is a general agreement that terrorism is bad and associated with nonacceptable, criminal behavior. Yet, there is a long history behind terrorist action, raising a multitude of definitional gray areas.

Historically, the term is of French origin, first used to describe the state-sponsored tactics employed by the Committee of Public Safety and the Revolutionary Tribunal under Robespierre's so-called *Regime de la Terreur* ("Reign of Terror"). Robespierre used terrorism as a national security strategy, which consisted of widespread surveillance and the threat and use of brutal, often lethal, tactics that deterred domestic anarchy. For Robespierre, *terrorisme* implied a sense of altruism and collective benefit, which resulted in nearly half a million arrests (by some estimates) and tens of thousands of dead French citizens.

While the term originated in relation to state-sponsored activities, in contemporary usage, terrorism is more commonly applied to the actions of individuals or nongovernmental groups. Yet, there is not a consistent definition in use around the world, which raises challenges for counterterrorism efforts. After the Sixtieth General Assembly of the United Nations convened in 2005, the representative for Iceland, Hjalmar Hannesson, concisely defined the dilemma posed by inconsistent definitions. He said, "nations had to come to agreement on a definition of the term 'terrorism,' for without a consensus of what constituted terrorism, nations could not unite against it."[1] The Malaysian Delegate Mohd Puad Zarkashi added that, "until all countries agreed on the enemy they sought to defeat, there would always be loopholes and safe havens for those criminals to escape justice and the rule of law."[2]

Even within the United States, there is a lack of agreement between government organizations on how to define terrorism.

- The FBI deems terrorism as "the unlawful use of force or violence against persons or property to intimidate or coerce a government, the civilian population, or any segment thereof, in furtherance of political or social objectives."[3]
- The U.S. Department of Defense defines it as "the calculated use of unlawful violence or threat of unlawful violence to inculcate fear; intended to coerce or to intimidate governments or societies in the pursuit of goals that are generally political, religious, or ideological."[4]

[1]United Nations General Assembly Press Release: *Agreed Definition of Term "Terrorism" Said to Be Needed for Consensus on Completing Comprehensive Convention Against It.* Department of Public Information, News and Media Division, New York. 7 July 2005.
[2]Ibid.
[3]United States Code of Federal Regulations: 28 C.F.R. Section 0.85.
[4]Terrorism Research. *What is Terrorism?* International Terrorism and Security Research.

- The Central Intelligence Agency considers terrorism to be "premeditated, politically motivated violence perpetrated against noncombatant targets by subnational groups or clandestine agents."[5]
- And different still, the Department of Homeland Security calls terrorism "any activity that involves an act that is dangerous to human life or potentially destructive to critical infrastructure or key resources, and is a violation of the criminal laws of the United States or of any state or other subdivision of the United States and appears to be intended to intimidate or coerce a civilian population to influence the policy of a government by intimidation or coercion, or to affect the conduct of a government by mass destruction, assassination, or kidnapping."[6]

There is equally no agreement on definition between noted academic experts. Inasmuch as there is a political dimension to terrorist behavior, there are also religious, sociological, and even psychological elements that play into how activity is employed and devised. Scholars from the myriad disciplines that have examined the phenomenon have yielded as many attempts at a definition.

To further muddy the definitional waters, media references to catastrophic events are often framed as terrorism before all the facts are known. A bombing of a building is not inherently terroristic; a narcotics cartel's violent tactics are not necessarily narco-terrorism; and the disruption of power to energy infrastructure is not *prima facie* cyberterrorism. Yet, current events are sometimes presented broadly as terrorist in nature, often to enhance the scope of the incident and consequently, the interest of concerned media consumers.

Taking into account these long-running deliberations over how to define terrorism, any comprehensive definition should be based on three important elements:

1. *The essence of the activity is the use or threatened use of violence.* Violence—actual or potential—supports one critical result of terrorism: fear. Citizens generally believe that their government has the

---

[5]Central Intelligence Agency. *CIA & The War on Terrorism—Terrorism FAQs.*

[6]Interestingly, DHS notes that "there is no one definition of terrorism accepted by the federal government, the definition may even vary within the United States Intelligence Community." United States Department of Homeland Security (10 November 2011). (*U/FOUO) Domestic Terrorism and Homegrown Violent Extremism Lexicon.* Office of Intelligence and Analysis.

capacity and capability to protect them, and violence that eludes the government protector shakes societal support for that government, and consequently, its policies and activities. The fear of violence is as effective in impacting government activity as violence itself.

2. *The targets of activity are civilians.* Under International Humanitarian Law (IHL), a civilian is a person who is not a member of his or her country's armed forces. An important element is that the act is purposely directed at civilians; actions that accidentally cause civilian casualties because individuals stumbled into an area of violent political activity are not necessarily terrorism.

3. *The objective of activity is political.* Terrorist action strives for specific ideological goals or political expectations, which can be centered on race, religion, national origin, or other systems of issue-oriented priorities. Implicitly, every ideology entails a political tendency, and thus, by its very nature, terrorism is also political.

1.2 WHAT IS VIOLENT EXTREMISM?

Extremism is a primary feature of terrorist behavior. It is an ideology or a viewpoint that is, as scholar Gus Martin writes, "radical in opinion, especially in political matters ... characterized by intolerance toward opposing interests and divergent opinions."[7] Violent extremism occurs when individuals or groups openly express their ideological beliefs through violence or a call for violence.

An important point is that while extremism may be a precursor to terrorism, ideological beliefs do not independently reach the threshold for an act of terrorism. There is a distinct difference between "terrorist" and "extremist" organizations. So long as extremist groups do not explicitly endorse violence, their beliefs and ideology are protected under the First Amendment to the U.S. Constitution.

Yet, the freedom and protections of speech, including overt "hate speech," present significant challenges for providing constitutional protections, for both people espousing biased opinions as well as for

---

[7]Martin, G. (2011). *Terrorism and Homeland Security.* SAGE Publications, Thousand Oaks, CA, p. 4.

those who may become victimized in furtherance of those subjective ideologies. The latter are in some cases called "hate crimes," which are deemed to have occurred when someone is targeted because of their perceived membership in a certain social group (race, religion, sexual orientation, etc.).

Understanding that advocating or using violence is central to the idea of violent extremism, it is important to clarify characteristics manifested by extremists writ large. Some of the most frequently occurring include:

- *Intolerance and superiority*: Extremists assume the moral high ground associated with their basic ideology. Most common are racial, religious and ethnic claims of superiority, which are espoused to illuminate their noble place in society. The overriding belief is that "the world is theirs," and the rest of the human race is fortunate to live in it and may continue to do so as long as they understand their place.
- *Otherism*: This is a presumption that a given social segment or group does not belong to the mainstream. It manifests in personal attacks that question one's motives, qualifications, experience or expertise. Social scientists call this "microaggression." Derogatory epithets such as hajji, kike, Mud people, referring to people of Middle Eastern, Jewish and non-European descent, respectively, are commonly used to label opponents while diverting attention from viewpoints opposed to the extremist ideology.
- *Absolutism*: Extremists embrace a Manichaean worldview—that is, one of moral, religious or philosophical dualism. Their position is one of moral absolutes, and their messages are designed to reinforce the notion that their opponents are "bad." This negates a need for discussion or debate on ideological validity because adversaries inherently have nothing in common. As a result, extremists view their own cause as noble while any opponents are necessarily always antagonistic.
- *Generalizations lacking foundation*: Extremists paint people, things and events with a broad brush, though lacking any evidence to support their claims. Rather than discuss facts and ideas that contradict these generalizations, extremists will simply ignore them, avoiding debate. This characteristic leads to false conclusions, which further the biased, ideological agenda.

- *Doomsday scenarios and conspiracy theories:* Extremists tend to describe an apocalyptic outcome from a failure to pursue their mission. This can include an invasion of the United States, an overthrow of the U.S. government by a foreign force, or the villainizing of the U.S. government itself. Conspiracy theories, such as the idea that the government was directly responsible for the 9/11 terrorist attacks, present a foundation and motivation for adhering to the extremist ideology in defense of the group.
- *Code speak*: Extremist groups use particular language to denigrate their opponents. Loaded terms and clichéd phrases help them quickly relay ideological beliefs without the need for critical thought or explanation. This bolsters confidence by reinforcing prejudices, as well as a sense of self-righteousness.

1.3 WHAT IS HOMEGROWN?

To best define the homegrown characteristic, it is useful to begin by defining what it is not. A general definition of international terrorism is a terrorist act committed against a foreign country by an actor not native to that country. Yet, an act of international terrorism does not require an actor to leave their native country. For example, an actor could target individuals with an international profile who are in the actor's home country, such as foreign ambassadors, tourists, business representatives or even academics.

Conversely, homegrown terrorists target individuals who are members or representatives of their own country. Timothy McVeigh, who parked a truck bomb in front of the Alfred P. Murrah Federal Building in Oklahoma City, killing 168 people and injuring 680 more, is an example.

Another critical element in determining international versus homegrown terrorism is where and when the attacker embraced their legitimizing ideology, as well as the intended political objectives. In that regard, an attacker's place of birth may not be the determining factor as it relates to classifying an attack and actor. A foreign national who immigrates to and resides in the United States for a period of time, and then embraces a violent extremist ideology with violent actions directed at Americans, is in fact homegrown. They may have started life elsewhere, but their life as a violent extremist is entirely American.

What is more, the birthplace of the ideology is not a criterion in determining homegrown versus international terrorism. The origin of the ideology is irrelevant; what matters is where it is embraced. For example, while an American or a long-term resident may swear allegiance to the al Qaeda ideology (which has its roots and much of its following on the international stage), if they pick up that terrorist banner and act within the United States, they are homegrown.

1.4 WHAT MOTIVATES HVE?

Regardless of different ideologies, nationalities, political objectives and targets (foreign and domestic), motivation for violent extremism generally arises from similar origins. Recognizing that there are always aberrations, HVE is most often driven by retribution or altruism. These powerful forces fit within a context of extremist ideology to propel individuals or groups into violent action.

The notion of retribution—near synonymous with a desire for revenge—is a rallying cry for the disenchanted who perceive a grave slight to those whom they identify as among their ideological group. Al Qaeda presents a perfect example. The U.S.-led war in Iraq came on top of a decades-long troubled history between dominant Western economies (i.e., American and European) and politically unstable Middle Eastern nations. Some Muslim ideologies (throughout the world) encapsulated these complex relationships in a derogatory narrative, positing that U.S. actions abroad were designed to oppress and kill Muslims.

For years, even before 9/11, Osama bin Laden was the most widely-known figure preaching this narrative, and he was clear in his motivation for attacking U.S. citizens, allies, and interests. In 2002, bin Laden published a letter, writing:

"Why are we fighting and opposing you? The answer is very simple:
1. *Because you attacked us and continue to attack us.*
   a. *You attacked us in Palestine.*
   b. *You attacked us in Somalia; you supported the Russian atrocities against us in Chechnya, the Indian oppression against us in Kashmir, and the Jewish aggression against us in Lebanon.*

   c. *Under your supervision, consent, and orders, the governments of our countries which act as your collaborators, attack us on a daily basis.*

   d. *You steal our wealth and oil at paltry prices because of your international influence and military threats. This theft is indeed the biggest theft ever witnessed by mankind in the history of the world.*

   e. *Your forces occupy our countries; you spread your military bases throughout them; you corrupt our lands, and you besiege our sanctuaries.*

2. *These tragedies and calamities are only a few examples of your oppression and aggression against us. It is commanded by our religion and intellect that the oppressed have a right to respond to aggression. Do not expect anything from us but jihad, resistance, and revenge. Is it in any way rational to expect that after America has attacked us for more than half a century that we will then leave her to live in security and peace?"*

His use of "us" in this case refers to the international Muslim community. While bin Laden and al Qaeda embraced a particularly vicious ideological bias, he and other members of the terrorist organization perceived their activities to be on behalf of a threatened global Muslim population. In this instance, the reason for the terrorist action was to exact retribution that could force a change in the U.S. government's actions. Bin Laden's letter continues:

   a. *The American people are the ones who pay the taxes which fund the planes that bomb us in Afghanistan, the tanks that strike and destroy our homes in Palestine, the armies which occupy our lands in the Arabian Gulf, and the fleets which endorse the blockade of Iraq. These tax dollars are given to Israel for it to continue attacking us and invade our lands.*

   b. *Also, the American army is part of the American people. It is the very same people who are shamelessly helping the Jews fight against us.*

   c. *The American people are the ones who employ both their men and their women in the American forces which attack us."*[8]

As retribution for U.S. government action, bin Laden employed violent extremism to encourage a political end, which aligns with the aforementioned definitions for terrorism. While al Qaeda was born abroad, and with regard to the United States, most of its adherents can be deemed international terrorists, this same desire for revenge is often the driving motivation for homegrown violence. It is not, however, the only motivation.

---

[8]Lawrence, B. (2005). *Messages to the World, The Statements of Osama bin Laden.*

Altruism is also a powerful motivation for HVE, albeit somewhat less obvious. Looking to regions where violent conflict is common, some violent extremists view their terrorist acts as a way of perpetuating a future safety for individual families, the cohesiveness of whole communities or the liberation of entire countries.

Israeli psychologist Ariel Merari identified and interviewed the social network surrounding Palestinian suicide attackers, including those whose detonation attempts had failed. He found that these individuals did not exhibit the characteristics of suicidal individuals (depression, alcohol or other drug abuse, signs of mental illness, etc.). Additionally, despite common assumptions, the terrorists did not often cite religion as a motivating factor in their planned or attempted attack. Rather, they viewed their action as a courageous method for advancing the cause from which their community or country could benefit. These clearly violent extremists were driven by a sense of altruism as it relates to the security concerns of their own societies.

A similar motivation is seen with Patriot Movement adherents, who cite the government's position on gun control legislation, welfare (and illegal immigration), abortion, same-sex marriage, and a lack of congressional fiscal responsibility as justification for potential civil unrest and state secession from the Union's activities.[9]

1.5 CONSIDERATIONS FOR ATTACK UTILITY

HVE and international terrorism are similar in many respects, and the overriding dynamic is anti-government. This can include opposition to U.S. foreign policy, though it might also be driven by adherence to religious, racial or other legitimizing ideologies. While the impetus for attack is rooted in beliefs, a terrorist's selection of how and where to attack is based on a consideration of utility. This is the estimate of an attack's consequences with respect to the intended target's value as a domestic or international interest and the political impact the attack will have on the intended audience.

[9]Republic Magazine (9 May 2013). *Civil Unrest and State Secession.*

Utility is a primary consideration for extremists during preparation for an attack, weighing desired results against the investment in activities to plan, rehearse and execute an operation. Always mindful of the aftermath, utility weighs heavily in the decision-making process of target selection, possible attack paths, methodologies and execution.

From the perspective of the attacker, fear provides a dual utility, enhancing terrorism's psychological impact. The first utility is that fear encourages societies to believe that, regardless of security investments, they will never be safe. The intent is to encourage a population to demand a change in whichever political activity a terrorist opposes.

The second utility is the persistent shaking of public confidence and trust in the security system, particularly because of "non-events"—those incidents that are highly publicized and scrutinized but that are largely anticlimactic. Examples of non-events include the 2006 liquid bomb plot, designed to destroy at least seven commercial airliners in flight traveling from the United Kingdom to the United States and Canada, or Pakistani-American Faisal Shahzad's 2010 attempted car bomb plot targeting New York City's Times Square. Persistent non-events occurring repeatedly and within the same specific infrastructure degrade trust and confidence in public-sector capabilities.

Yet, while counterterrorism professionals can assess the utility that HVE groups and individuals might find in a range of potential targets, continuing efforts to predictively model their decisions and consequential actions must include the inherently unpredictable and impossible-to-profile "Human Element." In an adversary, the Human Element describes that psychological component of unexpected or seemingly irrational decision making that is inherently human and impossible to replicate in a laboratory-generated simulation-based model. Despite the detection of HVE characteristics or behaviors, it is exceedingly difficult to anticipate a likely attack path.

While any terrorist attack is generally designed to induce widespread fear and uncertainty, attack utility often hinges on how it will affect three primary outcomes: critical infrastructure disruption; economic consequences; and psychological impact. Target selection and attack path methodologies seek to optimize the impact on these three potential outcomes. Critically, capitalizing on the reactive nature of the counterterrorism agencies and policies, even thwarted plots have realized the same benefits of a successful attack. Indeed, there is no such thing as a failed attack. To illustrate how HVE attacks can impact the three potential outcomes, consider these examples.

1.5.1 Critical Infrastructure Disruption—The DC Metro Plot

Critical infrastructure comprises systems and assets (physical or virtual) that are so vital to the United States that their failure or destruction would have an incapacitating and far-reaching impact on security, the economy, and/or public health and safety. The thwarted plot to bomb multiple Metrorail stations and hotels in the Washington, DC, area is an instructive example of the potential for overall system impact as a result of a design to maximize attack utility.

In 2010, Farooque Ahmed, a naturalized U.S. citizen born in Pakistan, was arrested for planning to bomb the Arlington Cemetery, Court House, Crystal City and Pentagon City metro stations. These stations were selected for a specific reason—Pentagon employees, largely uniformed military personnel, use them daily. Unlike previous rail attacks in Madrid (2004), London (2005) and Mumbai (2008), Ahmed "suggested using rolling suitcases rather than backpacks to kill as many people as possible."[10] This innovation on tactics is a perfect example of what is meant by "adaptive adversary."

According to the indictment filed after his arrest, Ahmed participated in surveillance and recorded video images of Metrorail stations on four occasions and forwarded the information on a thumb drive to a person he believed was an al Qaeda operative. Additionally, he planned to use at least one hotel that offered a vantage point for surveillance. The goal of the surveillance was to determine the security and busiest periods of all of the potential targets. The hotel itself may have provided an additional target.

While the plot was interrupted, the impact on the rail system could have been significant. The average weekday ridership for the Washington Metropolitan Area Transit Authority in 2010 was 750,654 passengers. The loss of life, injuries and economic consequences would have been devastating, to say nothing of the disruption to a critical

---

[10]Caldwell, A.A. (27 October 2010). *Farooque Ahmed Arrested for Plotting DC Terrorist Attack.* Huffington Post.

transportation system used by a sizeable population of government employees in the DC area.

Ahmed had all of the hallmark qualities of a homegrown terrorist. Educated in the United States, he earned a bachelor's degree in computer science from City University of New York and was pursuing a graduate degree online in risk management and data security at Aspen University.[11] He was employed as a contractor in Northern Virginia for Ericsson, a telecommunication company. Unlike some other U.S. citizens implicated in terror plots, Ahmed did not appear to have received overseas training from al Qaeda or any of its affiliates.[12]

1.5.2 Economic Consequences—The 9/11 Attacks

The economic impacts of the September 11, 2001, terror attacks were unprecedented. Following the attack, there was a 4-day shutdown of the aviation system. Estimates on the massive economic losses in trading, business productivity, revenue and jobs range widely. A sense of the scope of impact, however, can be gleaned from an academic study estimating the economic impacts of a hypothetical terrorist attack on the U.S. commercial air transport system.[13] The simulation modeled a 7-day shutdown of the entire U.S. commercial air transportation system, followed by a 2-year recovery period. The predicted losses ranged from $12.5 billion to $21.3 billion, with net system losses during the 24-month recovery ranging from $214 billion to $420 billion.[14]

The economic impact of 9/11 was instructive for violent extremists targeting the United States, and the ensuing prioritization of economic considerations in the terrorist decision-making phase was articulated in the November 2010 Special Issue of *Inspire* magazine, al Qaeda's online publication. An article entitled, "The Objective of Operation Hemorrhage," outlined the utility of asymmetric warfare against a superpower (i.e., the United States) and the expected security costs the country would bear to mitigate a new threat and associated risks. The *Inspire* "Letter from the Editor" advised, "This strategy of attacking the enemy with smaller but more frequent operations is what some

[11]Finn, P., Hsu, S.S., and Gibson, C. (28 October 2010). *Feds Arrest N.Va. Man in D.C. Metro Bomb Plot.* The Washington Post.
[12]Ibid.
[13]Gordon, P., Moore, J.E. II, Park, J.Y., et al. (2006). *The Economic Impacts of a Terrorist Attack on the U.S. Commercial Aviation System.*
[14]Ibid.

may refer to as the strategy of a thousand cuts. The aim is to bleed the enemy to death."[15]

1.5.3 Psychological Impact—The Mumbai Attacks

The first and most immediate effects of actual terror attacks are psychological.[16] Increased stress levels, decreased feelings of safety, heightened perceptions of threat and behavioral changes have all been noted in communities following terrorist incidents. Fear can influence decisions, alter lifestyles and affect entire cultures.

The November 26, 2008, attacks in Mumbai represent the potential of a terrorist trifecta—critical infrastructure disruption, economic consequences and psychological impact. The Mumbai attacks, also known as "26/11," consisted of 11 coordinated active shooter and bombing attacks across India's largest city. Ten heavily armed members of the Pakistan-based terrorist organization Lashkar-e-Taiba (LT) attacked a diverse collection of targets, holding the city, country, and the world hostage to their rampage for 3 days, killing 164 people and wounding at least 308.[17]

The immediate halt of all citizen and commercial movement throughout the city was expected and necessary. Yet, the city and the country showed remarkable resilience in the attack's aftermath. Rail service was fully restored the day after the incident ended, and flights into and out of Mumbai never stopped during the 60-plus hours of cleanup operation. Psychologically, it seems, Mumbai specifically, and India overall, was better prepared to deal with such a tragedy than was the United States in the aftermath of 9/11.[18]

Yet, as nations began to consider the potential impacts of violent extremism, the psychological outcome yielded a more global impact on the counterterrorism community. Several elements of the 26/11 attack demonstrated how terrorists could leverage strategy and tactics, given

[15]Al Qaeda in the Arabian Peninsula (November 2010). *The Objectives of Operation Hemorrhage, Inspire*, Issue 3. p 3.
[16]Waxman, D. (2011). *Living with terror, not living in terror: the impact of chronic terrorism on Israeli Society*. Perspectives on Terrorism—A Journal of the Terrorism Research Initiative. 5(5,6).
[17]Press Information Bureau—Government of India (11 December 2008). *HM Announces Measures to Enhance Security* (Press release).
[18]Panagaria, A. (29 November 2008). *The Economic Cost of the Mumbai Tragedy—Extrapolating from 9/11 and New York City*. Forbes.com.

appropriate intelligence information. For example, the Mumbai attackers used a military tactic known as "swarming" —using a decentralized force in a way that emphasizes mobility, communication, unit autonomy, and coordination or synchronization.[19] As a result, counterterrorism units around the world developed responses to this commando tactic, which was subsequently labeled a "Mumbai-style attack." The counterterrorism community came to recognize that such a tactic would be particularly devastating if executed by assailants possessing an intimate knowledge of the target by virtue of living or working near the location.

Fear of another Mumbai-style attack caught on quickly. In 2011, federal authorities warned hotels in major U.S. cities to be vigilant after intelligence indicated al Qaeda planned to launch a Mumbai-style attack on an upscale hotel in London.[20] Police agencies, such as the New York Police Department, began training to respond to this evolved tactic in drills simulating multiple bombs and shooters, as well as a bomb under a vehicle.[21] The Los Angeles Police Department responded by engaging in a combination of aggressive intelligence operations and community outreach.[22] The Mumbai attacks were a game changer on the local and international level.

With so many factors, motivations and targets associated with terrorism and violent extremism, there is hardly an academic discipline unattached to the issue of HVE. It is an emerging, crosscutting issue with which societies (democratic ones in particular) must come to grips. With a general appreciation for what HVE is, how extremists are motivated, and to what end, the next step is to discern the presence and scope of HVE in the United States and the groups that have long been engaged in domestic terrorism.

---

[19]Edwards, S.J.A. (2000). *Swarming on the Battlefield, Past, Present and Future.*
[20]Levine, M. and Griffin, J. (17 June 2011). *Hotels Warned of "Mumbai-style" Terror Threat.* Fox News.
[21]Esposito, R. and Eslocker, A. (14 October 2010). *As Terror Alert Continues, NYPD Holds Drill to Prep for Mumbai-Style Attack.* ABC News.
[22]Gertz, B. (11 April 2011). *L.A. Police Use Intel Networks Against Terror.* The Washington Times.

FURTHER READING

Ali, M.M., Blacker, J. and Jones, G. (April 2003). *Annual mortality rates and excess deaths of children under five in Iraq, 1991–98.* Population Studies. A Journal of Demography, Volume 57, Issue 2, 2003. http://www.tandfonline.com/doi/abs/10.1080/0032472032000097119?url_ver=Z39.88-2003&rfr_id=ori:rid:crossref.org&rfr_dat=cr_pub%3dpubmed#.Ufc_xxZy5UQ.

Allouni, T. [the Kabul correspondent of Al-Jazeera] (21 October 2001), transcript of an interview with Osama bin Laden, translated from Arabic by the Institute for Islamic Studies and Research (www.alneda.com).

al Qaeda in the Arabian Peninsula (November 2010) *The Objectives of Operation Hemorrhage,* Inspire, Issue 3.

Anti-Defamation League (1997). *Explosion of Hate: The Growing Danger of the National Alliance.* http://www.adl.org/explosion_of_hate/print.asp (Retrieved: 13 October 2012).

Anti-Defamation League (26 August 2008) *Two Sentenced in Los Angeles Terror Plot Against Jewish Institutions*: http://www.adl.org/main_Terrorism/los_angeles_sentenced.htm (Retrieved: 12 November 2012).

Associated Press/NBC New York (30 June 2011) *Man Accused of Flying from JFK to LA with Invalid Boarding Pass.* http://www.nbcnewyork.com/news/local/Invalid-Boarding-Pass-JFK-Los-Angeles-Atlanta-Arrest-124771394.html (Retrieved: 4 November 2012).

BBC News (14 November 2007). *One Bag Air Travel Rule Relaxed.* http://news.bbc.co.uk/2/hi/uk_news/7093795.stm (Retrieved: 29 October 2012).

BBC News (5 September 2006). *BA Says Terror Alert Cost It £40m.* http://news.bbc.co.uk/2/hi/business/5316920.stm (Retrieved: 29 October 2012).

BBC News (7 September 2006). *Security Alert Cost Easyjet £4m.* http://news.bbc.co.uk/2/hi/business/5323082.stm (Retrieved: 29 October 2012).

Berman, E. (2009). *Radical, Religious and Violent: The New Economics of Terrorism.* MIT Press.

Bleich, A., Gelkopf, M. and Solomon, Z. (2003). *Exposure to terrorism, stress-related mental health symptoms, and coping behaviors among a nationally representative sample in Israel.* JAMA, 290, 612–620.

Bockstette, C. (2008). *Jihadist Terrorist Use of Strategic Communication Management Techniques. George C. Marshall Center Occasional Paper Series* (20). http://www.marshallcenter.org/mcpublicweb/MCDocs/files/College/F_Publications/occPapers/occ-paper_20-en.pdf (Retrieved: 30 September 2012).

Bosworth, Jr., C. (15 March 1998). *Illinois Man Sought Start of Race War, Source Says.* St. Louis Post-Dispatch (Louis Post-Dispatch, Inc.): p. A1.

B'Tselem-Statistics—Fatalities 29 September 2000–15 January 2005: http://old.btselem.org/statistics/english/Casualties.asp?sD = 29&sM = 09&sY = 2000&eD = 15&eM = 1&eY = 2005&filterby = event &oferet_stat = before (Retrieved: 11 November 2012).

Caldwell, Alicia A (27 October 2010). *Farooque Ahmed Arrested for Plotting DC Terrorist Attack.* Huffington Post.

CBS News (6 January 2010). *Indictment in U.S. v. Abdulmutallab.* http://www.cbsnews.com/htdocs/pdf/Abdulmutallab_Indictment.pdf (Retrieved: 3 November 2012).

Central Intelligence Agency. *CIA & The War on Terrorism—Terrorism FAQs.* https://www.cia.gov/news-information/cia-the-war-on-terrorism/terrorism-faqs.html (Retrieved; 29 September 2012).

"Civilian" http://dictionary.reference.com/etymology/civilian (Retrieved: 30 September 2012).

Clarke, R.A. (2004). *Against All Enemies, Inside America's War on Terror.* Free Press.

Clutterbuck, Lindsey (30 November 2008). *Terrorists Have to Be Lucky Once; Targets, Every Time.* RAND: http://www.rand.org/commentary/2008/11/30/DNA.html (Retrieved: 30 September 2012).

CNN Justice (9 October 2012). *Passenger Clad in Body Armor Arrested for Transporting Smoke Bomb.* http://www.cnn.com/2012/10/09/justice/california-hazardous-materials-airport-arrest/index.html (Retrieved: 4 November 2012).

CNN Travel (15 March 2012). *Denver Airport Concourse Evacuated.* http://articles.cnn.com/2002-03-15/travel/denver.evacuation_1_concourse-rescreened-security-breach?_s = PM:TRAVEL (Retrieved: 4 November 2012).

CNN Travel (6 January 2010). *TSA Takes Responsibility for Newark Airport Breach.* http://articles.cnn.com/2010-01-06/travel/new.jersey.security.breach_1_security-breach-tsa-officials-area-airports?_s = PM:TRAVEL (Retrieved: 4 November 2012).

CNN U.S. (28 April 1997). *Turner Diaries Introduced in McVeigh Trial.* http://articles.cnn.com/1997-04-28/us/9704_28_okc_1_timothy-mcveigh-mcveigh-trial-oklahoma-state-trooper?_s = PM:US (Retrieved: 27 October 2012).

CNN U.S. (18 February 2012). *"Total Misunderstanding" Causes Plane to Return to New York.* http://articles.cnn.com/2002-02-18/us/gen.plane.security_1_security-breach-rescreened-plane?_s = PM:US (Retrieved: 4 November 2012).

CNN U.S. (13 March 2008). *Hussein's Iraq and al Qaeda Not Linked, Pentagon Says.* http://articles.cnn.com/2008-03-13/us/alqaeda.saddam_1_qaeda-targets-of-iraqi-state-iraqi-state-terror-operations?_s = PM:US (Retrieved: 13 November 2012).

Cozzens, J.B. and Rosenau, W. (15 August 2009). *Training for Terror: The "Homegrown" Case of Jami at al-Islam al-Sahih.* Combating Terrorism Center at West Point. http://www.ctc.usma.edu/posts/training-for-terror-the-"homegrown"-case-of-jamiat-al-islam-al-sahih (Retrieved: 12 November 2012).

Discovery Channel Production (2003). *Searching for the Roots of 9/11.* http://ffh.films.com/id/6492/Searching_for_the_Roots_of_911.htm (Retrieved: 11 November 2012).

Eagleton, Terry (1991). *Ideology: An Introduction.* Verso.

Eckstein, Z. and Tsiddon, D. (March 2004). *Macroeconomic Consequences of Terror: Theory and the Case of Israel.* The Foerder Institute for Economic Research and The Sackler Institute of Economic Studies: http://econ.tau.ac.il/papers/foerder/7-2004.pdf (Retrieved: 11 November 2012).

Exhibit Document 259-6 (14 December 2007). *Blueprint 2005.* Case 8:05-cr-00214-CJC: http://www.investigativeproject.org/documents/case_docs/536.pdf (Retrieved: 12 November 2012).

Edwards, S.J.A. (2000). *Swarming on the Battlefield, Past, Present and Future.* RAND Monograph MR-1100. RAND Corporation.

Esposito, R. and Eslocker, A. (14 October 2010). *As Terror Alert Continues, NYPD Holds Drill to Prep for Mumbai Style Attack.* ABC News: http://abcnews.go.com/Blotter/terror-alert-continues-nypd-holds-drill-prep-mumbai/story?id = 11879452#.UKAeZI5y5UR.

Evelyn, Columba Sara (2011). *Italicus Express Bombing 1974.* Fec Publishing.

"Extremism"—Oath Keepers and Three Percenters Part of Growing Anti-Government Movement. Anti-Defamation League. http://www.adl.org/main_Extremism/oath_keepers_three_percenters.htm (Retrieved: 23 October 2012).

FBI, Los Angeles Division (6 March 2009). *Man Who Formed Terrorist Group That Plotted Attacks on Military and Jewish Facilities Sentenced to 16 Years in Federal Prison.* http://www.fbi.gov/losangeles/press-releases/2009/la030609ausa.htm (Retrieved: 12 November 2012).

Feuer, A. (15 February 2001). *Bin Laden Pilot Says He Helped Buy Jet to Ship Missiles.* The New York Times: http://www.nytimes.com/2001/02/15/nyregion/bin-laden-pilot-says-he-helped-buy-jet-to-ship-missiles.html (Retrieved: 10 November 2012).

Faturechi, R. and Winton, R. (18 April 2010). *White Supremacist Rally at L.A. City Hall Draws Violent Counter-Protest*: http://articles.latimes.com/print/2010/apr/18/local/la-me-white-supremacist18-2010apr18 (Retrieved 7 October 2012).

Finn, P., Hsu, S.S. and Gibson, C. (28 October 2010). *Feds Arrest N. Va. Man in D.C. Metro Bomb Plot*. The Washington Post.

Ganor, B. (2005). *The Counter-Terrorism Puzzle, A Guide for Decision Makers*. Transaction Publishers, Rutgers, Piscataway, NJ.

Ganor, B. *Defining Terrorism—Is One Man's Terrorist Another Man's Freedom Fighter?* IDC Herzliya, International Institute for Counter-Terrorism, Research and Publications. http://www.ict. org.il/ResearchPublications/tabid/64/Articlsid/432/Default.aspx (Retrieved: 28 September 2012).

Gertz, Bill (11 April 2011). *L.A. Police Use Intel Networks Against Terror*. The Washington Times. http://www.washingtontimes.com/news/2011/apr/11/la-police-use-intel-networks-against-terror/ (Retrieved: 11 November 2012).

Gordon, P., Moore, J.E., II, Park, J.Y., et al. (2006). *The Economic Impacts of a Terrorist Attack on the U.S. Commercial Aviation System*. University of Southern California, http://www-bcf.usc. edu/~pgordon/pdf/200609riskanalysis.pdf (Retrieved 29 October 2012).

Hajela, D. (19 August 2011). *For Some, Post-9/11 Life Meant Leaving NYC*. Huffington Post, http://www.huffingtonpost.com/2011/08/19/for-some-post911-life-mea_n_931420.html?view = print&comm_ref = false (Retrieved: 10 November 2012).

Hamm, M.S. (27 October 2008). *Prisoner Radicalization: Assessing the Threat in U.S. Correctional Institutions*. U.S. Department of Justice Programs, National Institute of Justice, The Research, Development, and Evaluation Agency of the U.S. Department of Justice, http://www. nij.gov/nij/journals/261/prisoner-radicalization.htm (Retrieved: 12 November 2012).

Harris, R. (10 October 2006). *Kevin James and the JIS Conspiracy*. The Enemy Within, FRONTLINE. http://www.pbs.org/wgbh/pages/frontline/enemywithin/reality/james.html (Retrieved: 12 November 2012).

Hoffman, B. (1998). *Inside Terrorism*. Columbia University Press.

Hoffman, B. (2006). *Inside Terrorism* (2nd ed.). Columbia University Press.

Huddy, L., Feldman, S., Capelos, T., et al. (2002). *The consequences of terrorism: disentangling the effects of personal and national threat*. Political Psychology, 23, 485–509.

ICRC. *What Is International Humanitarian Law?* http://www.icrc.org/eng/resources/documents/legal-fact-sheet/humanitarian-law-factsheet.htm? (Retrieved: 30 September 2012).

ICRC. *Protocol Additional to the Geneva Conventions of 12 August 1949, and Relating to the Protection of Victims of International Armed Conflicts (Protocol I), 8 June 1977*. International Humanitarian Law—Treaties & Documents. http://www.icrc.org/ihl.nsf/full/470?opendocument (Retrieved: 30 September 2012).

Iggulden, Amy (26 August 2006). *Ryanair Sues Government over "Insane" Security at Airports*. The Telegraph. http://www.telegraph.co.uk/news/1527286/Ryanair-sues-Government-over-insane-security-at-airports.html (Retrieved: 29 October 2012).

"International Terrorism" The Free Dictionary. http://www.thefreedictionary.com/international + terrorism (Retrieved: 26 October 2012).

Iyad, A. (1983). *Without a Homeland*. Tel-Aviv, Mifras.

Jenkins, B.M. (1975). International terrorism: a new mode of conflict. In D. Carlton and C. Schaerf (Eds.), *International Terrorism and World Security*. Croom Helm, London.

James, S. (22 August 2006). *UK Terror Scare: Airlines Threaten Legal Action Against British Government*. World Socialist website. http://www.wsws.org/articles/2006/aug2006/terr-a22.shtml (Retrieved: 29 October 2012).

Jewish Virtual Library. *Definitions of Terrorism*. A Division of the American-Israeli Cooperative Enterprise. http://www.jewishvirtuallibrary.org/jsource/Terrorism/terrordef.html (Retrieved: 28 September 2012).

JSOnline (3 August 2007). *Ex-cop Linked to Rogue Group.* Milwaukee—Wisconsin Journal Sentinel. http://www.jsonline.com/news/milwaukee/29376044.html (Retrieved: 27 October 2012).

King, W. (21 August 1990). *Books of The Times; A Farmer's Fatal Obsession With Jews and Taxes.* The New York Times. http://www.nytimes.com/1990/08/21/books/books-of-the-times-a-farmer-s-fatal-obsession-with-jews-and-taxes.html (Retrieved: 23 October 2012).

Laing, K. (3 May 2012). *Sen. Ran Paul Pushes Online Petition to "End the TSA."* The Hill's Transportation. http://thehill.com/blogs/transportation-report/tsa/225359-sen-paul-launches-petition-to-end-the-tsa- (Retrieved: 10 November 2012).

Laqueur, W. *Terrorism: A Brief History.* E-Journal USA. http://www.laqueur.net/index2.php?r = 2&id = 71 (Retrieved: 28 September 2012).

Laville, S. (19 August 2006). *Five key questions for anti-terror investigation.* The Guardian. http://www.guardian.co.uk/uk/2006/aug/19/terrorism.worl (Retrieved: 28 October 2012).

Lawrence, B. (2005). *Messages to the World, the Statements of Osama bin Laden.* Verso, London—New York.

Levine, M. and J. Griffin (17 June 2011). *Hotels Warned of Mumbai-Style Terror Threat.* Fox News. http://www.foxnews.com/politics/2011/06/16/hotels-warned-mumbai-style-terror-threat/ (Retrieved: 11 November 2012).

Linton, M. *The Terror in the French Revolution.* Kingston University (Retrieved: 29 September 2012).

Mackey, R. (20 November 2009). *Can Soldiers Be the Victims of Terrorism?* The New York Times. http://thelede.blogs.nytimes.com/2009/11/20/define-terrorism/ (Retrieved: 29 September 2012).

Martin, G. (2011). *Terrorism and Homeland Security.* SAGE Publications, Thousand Oaks, California.

Maslow, A.H. (1943). *A theory of human motivation.* Psychological Review, 50(4), 370–396.

McDonald, A. (1978). *The Turner Diaries.* Barricade Books, Inc., Fort Lee, NJ.

McLagan, G. (30 June 2000). *Panorama Special—The Nailbomber.* http://news.bbc.co.uk/2/hi/programmes/panorama/archive/811720.stm (Retrieved: 27 October 2012).

Miller, Phil (23 February 2000). *Black Man's Killer Said: "We're Starting the Turner Diaries Early".* The Scotsman (The Scotsman Publications), p. 3.

Moore, John. *The Evolution of Islamic Terrorism an Overview.* PBS Frontline. http://www.pbs.org/wgbh/pages/frontline/shows/target/etc/modern.html (Retrieved: 11 November 2012).

Moore, R. (2005). *Cybercrime: Investigating High Technology Computer Crime.* Matthew Bender & Company, p. 258.

Mueller, J. and Stewart, M.G. (2 April 2010). *Hardly Existential: Thinking Rationally About Terrorism.* Foreign Affairs.

National Commission on Terrorist Attacks Upon the United States (22 July 2004). *Appendix A: The Financing of the 9/11 Plot.* http://govinfo.library.unt.edu/911/staff_statements/911_TerrFin_App.pdf (Retrieved: 29 October 2012).

National Security Council Memorandum for Condoleeza Rice, from Richard A. Clarke (25 January 2001) *Presidential Policy Initiative/Review—the al Qaeda Network.* Declassified: 7 April 2004: http://www2.gwu.edu/~nsarchiv/NSAEBB/NSAEBB147/clarke%20memo.pdf (Retrieved: 11 November 2012).

National Socialist Movement website: http://www.nsm88.org/aboutus.html (Retrieved: 7 October 2012).

National Socialist Movement website: *NSM—after Action Report from Los Angeles.* http://www.nsm88.org/reports/nsmnationals2010.htm (Retrieved: 7 October 2012).

Naughton, P. and Adam, S. (11 August 2006). *Terror May Already be Priced into Values*. The Times (London). Archived: http://www.webcitation.org/5whHxCEAT from original article. (Retrieved 29 October 2012).

Netanyahu, B. (1986). *Terrorism: How the West Can Win*. Farrar, Straus & Giroux.

Netanyahu, B. (1996). *Fighting Terrorism. How Democracies Can Defeat Domestic and International Terrorists*. Allison and Busby.

New York Times (21 April 1995). *White Supremacist Executed for Murdering 2 in Arkansas*. http://www.nytimes.com/1995/04/21/us/white-supremacist-executed-for-murdering-2-in-arkansas.html (Retrieved: 23 November 2012).

Noble, K. (1998). *Tabernacle of Hate, Why They Bombed Oklahoma City*. Voyager Publishing.

Norton-Taylor, R. and O. Bowcott *"Mumbai-Style"Terror Attack on UK, France and Germany Foiled*. The Guardian. http://www.guardian.co.uk/world/2010/sep/29/terror-attack-plot-europe-foiled (Retrieved: 11 November 2012).

Panagaria, A. (29 November 2008) *The Economic Cost of the Mumbai Tragedy—Extrapolating from 9/11 and New York City*. Forbes.com: http://www.forbes.com/2008/11/29/mumbai-economic-cost-oped-cx_ap_1129panagariya.html (Retrieved: 11 November 2012).

Press Information Bureau—Government of India (11 December 2008). *HM Announces Measures to Enhance Security* (Press release). http://pib.nic.in/newsite/erelease.aspx?relid = 45446 (Retrieved: 11 November 2012).

Reiff, M.R. (April 2008) *Terrorism, Retribution and Collective Responsibility*. Social Theory and Practice. Tallahassee, Vol. 34. http://www.omnilogos.com/2011/06/15/terrorism-retribution-and-collective-responsibility/ (Retrieved: 11 November 2012).

Republic Magazine (9 May 2013). *Civil Unrest and State Secession*. http://www.republicmagazine.com/news/civil-unrest-and-state-secession.html (Retrieved 14 May 2013).

"Retribution" Merriam Webster Dictionary: http://www.merriam-webster.com/dictionary/retribution (Retrieved: 26 October 2012).

Richardson, L. (2006). *What Terrorists Want, Understanding the Enemy, Containing the Threat*. Random House, New York, NY.

Schuster, M.A., Stein, B.D., Jaycox, L.H., et al. (2001). *A national survey of stress reactions after the September 11, 2001, terrorist attacks*. New England Journal of Medicine, 345, 1507–1512.

Scheuer, M. (2004). Imperial Hubris. Dulles, Virginia: Brassey's, Inc.

Schroeder, S. (5 November 2012). *Symantec and Others Hacked by Anonymous*. http://mashable.com/2012/11/05/paypal-symantec-and-others-hacked-by-anonymous/ (Retrieved: 10 November 2012).

Shariat, S. Mallonee, S. and Stephens-Stidham, S. (December 1998). *Summary of Reportable Injuries in Oklahoma*. Oklahoma State Department of Health. http://web.archive.org/web/20080110063748/http://www.health.state.ok.us/PROGRAM/injury/Summary/bomb/OKCbomb.htm (Retrieved: 13 October 2012).

Siegel, H. and Lee C.E., (25 December 2010). *"High explosive"—U.S. Charges Abdulmutallab*. Politico. http://www.politico.com/news/stories/1209/30973.html (Retrieved: 3 November 2012).

Sinclair, S.J. and Antonius, D. (2012). *The Psychology of Terrorism Fears*. Oxford University Press.

Sipsey Street Irregulars. *"What is a "Three Percenter?"*http://sipseystreetirregulars.blogspot.com/2009/02/what-is-three-percenter.html (Retrieved: 23 October 2012).

Smith, K. (15 June 2011) *The Threat of Muslim-American Radicalization in U.S. Prisons*. Testimony presented before the U.S. House of Representatives, Committee on Homeland Security. http://homeland.house.gov/sites/homeland.house.gov/files/Testimony%20Smith_1.pdf (Retrieved: 12 November 2012).

Southern Poverty Law Center. *Inspired by Neo-Nazi Tracts, Youth's Rampage Ends in Death.* http://www.splcenter.org/get-informed/intelligence-report/browse-all-issues/2006/spring/neo-nazi-murder (Retrieved: 27 October 2012).

START—National Consortium for the Study of Terrorism and Responses to Terrorism. *Terrorist Organization Profile: Covenant Sword and Arm of the Lord (CSA).* http://www.start.umd.edu/start/data_collections/tops/terrorist_organization_profile.asp?id = 3226 (Retrieved: 13 October 2012).

Stern, J. (2004). *Terror in the Name of God, Why Religious Militants Kill.* Harper Collins Publishers, New York, NY.

Stone, M. (16 April 2012). *Anonymous Takes Down CIA, DOJ, FBI, NASA, MI6.* Examiner.com. http://www.examiner.com/article/anonymous-takes-down-cia-doj-fbi-nasa-mi6   (Retrieved: 10 November 2012).

Stotzer, R. (2007). *Comparison of Hate Crime Rates Across Protected and Unprotected Groups.* UCLA, Williams Institute: http://escholarship.org/uc/item/4c21d67t (Retrieved: 7 October 2012).

"Terrorism," Encyclopedia Britannica. p. 3 (Retrieved: 28 September 2012).

Terrorism Research. *What Is Terrorism?* International Terrorism and Security Research. http://www.terrorism-research.com/ (Retrieved: 29 September 2012).

The Constitution of the United States (2005), National Center for Constitutional Studies, Malta, ID, Second Edition.

"Three Percenter" Urban Dictionary. http://www.urbandictionary.com/define.php?term = three%20percenter (Retrieved: 23 October 2012).

Touré (2011). *Who's Afraid of Post-Blackness? What It Means to Be Black Now.* Free Press, New York, NY.

Tucker, R.C. (1978). *The Marx-Engels Reader.* W. W. Norton & Company.

United Nations General Assembly Press Release. *Agreed Definition of Term 'Terrorism' Said to Be Needed for Consensus on Completing Comprehensive Convention Against It.* Department of Public Information, News and Media Division, New York. 7 July 2005.

von Winterfeldt, D. and O'Sullivan, T. (June 2006). *Should We Protect Commercial Airplanes Against Surface-to-Air Missile Attacks by Terrorists?.* Decision Analysis, 3(2), 63–75.

Public Information, News and Media Division, New York. 7 July 2005. http://www.un.org/News/Press/docs/2005/gal3276.doc.htm (Retrieved: 29 September 2012).

USA Patriot Act of 2001 (42 U.S.C. 5195c(e) Section 1016 (e)).

United States Code of Federal Regulations: 28 C.F.R. Section 0.85.

USA Today. Associated Press. 20 June 2001. *Victims of the Oklahoma City Bombing.* http://usatoday30.usatoday.com/news/nation/2001-06-11-mcveigh-victims.htm (Retrieved: 13 October 13, 2012).

Waxman, D. (2011). *Living with terror, not living in terror: the impact of chronic terrorism on Israeli Society.* Perspectives on Terrorism—a Journal of the Terrorism Research Initiative. 5(5,6).

Whitaker, D.J. (Ed.) (2001). *The Terrorism Reader* Routledge, New York, NY.

Wilcox, L. (1997). *The Watchdogs: A Close Look At Anti-Racist "Watchdog" Groups.* Self-published through Editorial Research Service.

Wilcox, L. (1996). What is Extremism? Style and tactics matter more than goals. In J. George and L.W. Amherst (Eds.), *American Extremists: Militias, Supremacists, Klansmen, Communists and Others.* Prometheus, New York, NY.

Wilcox, L. *Laird Wilcox on Extremist Traits.* http://www.lairdwilcox.com/news/hoaxerproject.html (Retrieved: 7 October 2012).

CHAPTER 2

Ideological Motivation

The Department of Homeland Security (DHS) report, "Rightwing Extremism: Current Economic and Political Climate Fueling Resurgence in Radicalization and Recruitment," was leaked in 2009.[1] The report was coordinated by the FBI and prepared by the DHS Extremism and Radicalization Branch, Homeland Environment Threat Analysis Division, which studied domestic terrorism, neo-Nazis, and white supremacists. It noted that white supremacist and violent anti-government groups could potentially be pushed beyond rhetoric as the recent financial crisis and election of the first African-American president offered unprecedented impetus for rightwing radicalization and recruitment.

Citing the example of Timothy McVeigh, the report suggested that "the possible passage of new restrictions on firearms and the return of military veterans facing significant challenges reintegrating into their communities could lead to the potential emergence of terrorist groups or lone wolf extremists capable of carrying out violent attacks."

In the ensuing political firestorm, given the perceived focus on all veterans, DHS Secretary Janet Napolitano withdrew the report, explaining that the threat was limited to a small number of returning soldiers. Yet, the reality is that the report did not state that conservatives or veterans are a "suspect" class. Rather, the report revealed that white supremacist groups are interested in returning veterans because of their skills. While the DHS report became politically charged, its findings were congruous with previous studies indicating that every year in the United States (with the exception of 2001), right-wing extremism is responsible for more instances of violence than Islamic extremism.[2]

The New America Foundation published a subsequent report, determining that while the law enforcement focus on "jihadi groups" was appropriate in the aftermath of 9/11, today, the scope should be

---

[1]U.S. Department of Homeland Security Assessment (7 April 2009). *Rightwing Extremism: Current Economic and Political Climate Fueling Resurgence in Radicalization and Recruitment.*
[2]Center for American Progress—Think Progress (19 April 2012). *CHART: 17 Years After Oklahoma City Bombing, Right-Wing Extremism Is Significant Domestic Terror Threat.*

broadened to include "nonjihadist" extremists.[3] Nonjihadists are defined as right-wing and left-wing extremists who oppose the government, as well as neo-Nazis, anti-Gay, anti-abortion, and violent animal and environmental activists. The report found that from September 2001 through September 2012, jihadist and nonjihadist terrorists killed about the same number of people in the United States. Nonjihadist extremists, however, committed 10 attacks, while jihadists committed just four. More than 60% of the 127 people indicted on terrorism-related weapons charges were nonjihadist, and there were 11 anarchists, white supremacist, or right-wing extremists indicted for possessing chemical or biological materials. Meanwhile, no jihadist terrorists have acquired chemical or biological weapons nor are any publically known to have tried to acquire them.

Despite the increasing threat from nonjihadist groups, there has been a continued outsized focus on jihadists as the exclusive HVE risk to the United States. There are numerous extremist groups embracing a range of doctrines, while many groups and individuals bond with more than one ideological proclivity. Given this broad range of ideologies and factions, the growing HVE threat demands a more comprehensive categorization of extremist groups in the United States. There are numerous examples, and these are best understood from the perspectives of three ideological motivations: race, religion, and issue orientation.

2.1 RACIAL IDEOLOGY

Extremist organizations founded on racial lines have a long history in the United States. The post-9/11 era in particular has yielded an increase in associated rhetoric or "hate speech" and responses in recruitment and membership. The race category refers to groups and associated individuals espousing racial supremacy as the foundation of their ideological principles (recognizing that groups and individuals may embrace philosophies that cross over into other categories, such as religion).

Nearly half of the 6,222 hate crimes reported in 2011 were racially motivated, according to FBI figures, with nearly three-fourths directed at African-Americans. Meanwhile, more than 16% of hate

[3]Bergen, P. and Rowland, J. (11 September 2012). *11 Years After 9/11: Who Are the Terrorists?* CNN Opinion.

crimes were driven by an anti-white bias.[4] This level of racial extremism can be traced to the primary drivers described in the aforementioned DHS report—a challenging economy and an African-American president.

Interestingly, extremists and scholars alike cite recent economic dislocations, as well as political and cultural developments, as the impetuses for increasing racial polarity and interest in extremist organizations. August Kreis, who resigned as leader of an Aryan Nations faction after his conviction on veteran's benefits fraud, explained, "The worse the economy gets, the more the groups are going to grow ... White people are arming themselves − and black people too. I believe eventually it's going to come down to civil war."[5]

At the same time, one of the most galvanizing forces for racial extremists (as well as across religion and issue-oriented categories) was "the Obama factor;" that is, the tectonic shifts in American politics that allowed a black man with a foreign-sounding name and a Muslim-born father to occupy the Oval Office. He became a rallying symbol for racial identity adherents, and the extremist intolerance and conspiratorial perceptions were further enhanced when the president appointed Rahm Emanuel as White House Chief of Staff. This was a nightmare scenario for many racial ideologues, as the so-called Zionist Occupied Government (ZOG) was in the hands of an African American and a Modern Orthodox Jew. Within his first 8 months in office, President Obama became the target of more than 30 death threats a day, a 400% increase from about 3,000 a year during the George W. Bush Administration.[6]

The growing interest and fellowship in numerous extremist groups present significant challenges for efforts to counter and prevent HVE. While racial ideological groups are numerous, some of the most prevalent include the following.

[4]Ryan, D. (10 December 2012). *Hate Crimes Down in 2011, but Anti-Gay Violence Up, FBI Says.* The Los Angeles Times.
[5]Intelligence Report (2012). *The Year in Hate and Extremism, The "Patriot" Movement Explodes.* The Southern Poverty Law Center. Spring 2012/Issue 145.
[6]Harnden, T. (3 August 2009). *Barack Obama Faces 30 Death Threats a Day, Stretching US Secret Service.* The Telegraph.

2.1.1 Black Separatists

These are groups whose ideologies include principles of racially based hatred, black supremacy and/or black separatist ideologies. Although these groups increasingly claim doctrines that seem to exempt them from the laws of the land, racial superiority dominates their ideology. Black separatist groups can be found across the nation, with the Nation of Islam and the New Black Panther Party (NBPP) being most prevalent.

The Nation of Islam arose from the preaching of Elijah Poole, later titled the Honorable Elijah Muhammad, in Detroit. It was founded on the general themes of peace and harmony, with an emphasis on religion and the importance of God. Academic and social priorities were placed on mathematics and respect for the law, respectively, and in that regard, it was specifically affirmed that one is never to be armed or to engage in war as the aggressor, for to do so is contrary to what was deemed righteous.

Elijah Muhammad's son, Warith Deen Mohammed, was declared the Nation's leader after his father's death. He instituted a number of substantial changes, embracing a more traditional interpretation of Islam (largely Sunni) and notably welcomed white worshippers while also reaching out to Christians and Jews. Louis Farrakhan (born Louis Eugene Wolcott) converted to Nation of Islam and quickly rose through the ranks, becoming an assistant minister after only 9 months. He later became the official spokesperson for the Nation until Elijah Muhammad's death in 1975.

In 1978, however, following Warith Deen Mohammed's organizational changes, Farrakhan decided to walk away from the Nation with the intention of restoring the group to its original foundation and purpose. He became increasingly anti-government, anti-Semitic, homophobic and racist. Although Farrakhan has often come out against violence in the black community, he can hardly be embraced as a beacon of peace and love. His willingness to denigrate other races, religions and people of differing sexual orientations clearly illustrates an intolerant ideology emblematic of extremist organizations.

2.1.2 New Black Panther Party

The NBPP or Black Panther Party for Self-Defense was founded in Dallas, Texas, in 1989. The NBPP ideology endorses revolution and black unity based on self-determination, drawing on a socialist doctrine known as collective economics. Unlike the original Black Panther Party, the NBPP is anti-white, anti-Semitic and embraces what is essentially a Black supremacy platform.

The NBPP advocates a separate nation that will allow members to, among other things, implement their own laws, provide reparations to African-Americans for slavery and win the freedom of incarcerated black inmates. Although reportedly small in size (claiming a few thousand members across the country), they avail themselves of media opportunities by making racist, anti-Semitic pronouncements.[7]

Characteristic of extremist organizations, the NBPP embraces some conspiracy theories similar to their neo-Nazi and white supremacist counterparts, most notably, that Jews received advance warning of the 9/11 attacks. Unlike some extremist organizations, however, the NBPP does not shy away from advocating violence. In March 2012, after placing a $10,000 bounty on the head of George Zimmerman (a white Sanford, Florida, neighborhood watch volunteer who killed 17-year-old African-American Trayvon Martin), the NBPP held a press conference, circulating "wanted dead or alive" posters for Zimmerman.[8]

2.1.3 Ku Klux Klan

Founded in 1865, the Ku Klux Klan's (KKK) primary advocacy centers on white supremacy and white nationalism, but it also includes anti-Semitic, anti-Catholic, anti-immigrant, and homophobic ideologies, as well as Nativism and Neo-Confederate beliefs. Current documented KKK locations show a presence across the southern states and in the Great Lakes region. There are two or fewer documented KKK chapters in each of 30 states, with a declining number of chapters and membership.[9] Cross burnings largely go unreported, although their significance as a fear and violence-based strategy of terror via intimidation harkens back to the lynching and church bombing of the civil rights era.

Evidence of a reinvigorated Klan and their trepidation over "the Obama factor" emerged just 2 days after the President's re-election,

---

[7]Southern Poverty Law Center. *New Black Panther Party*.
[8]Pulaski, R. (23 March 2012). *New Black Panther Party Issues "Wanted Dead or Alive" Posters for George Zimmerman*. US Message Board.
[9]Southern Poverty Law Center. *Hate Map*.

when The Knight's Party website stated: "This election has offered positive proof that white Christian people have lost control of this former Republic. Contrary to what you have been taught in school and in church, America was founded as a White Christian homeland."[10]

2.1.4 Neo-Confederates

These are groups that seek to return to the racist principles of the pre-Civil War South. The foundation of the neo-Confederate movement is to honor the Confederate States of America and veterans of the Confederacy, as established during the U.S. Civil War. Neo-Confederates believe they preserve the true spirit of the Union, with the Confederacy being a rational, legitimate successor to the original government borne of the American Revolution. Some neo-Confederates view the Civil War as a conflict between a secular North and a Christian South.[11]

The heart of the neo-Confederate movement, largely represented by the Alabama-based League of the South (LOS), is reportedly decreasing in membership, with chapters in 16 states.[12] Yet, the group is also becoming more radical.[13] The LOS opposes racial diversity, particularly racial intermarriage, and seeks to establish a society composed of "general European cultural hegemony."[14] Michael Hill first established LOS at the University of Alabama, his alma mater, and the group's ultimate political goal of a "free and independent Southern republic" seeks to legitimize their ideological efforts.

In a 2012 essay, Hill claimed that white people are endowed with a "God-ordained superiority." Whites of "honor, genius and principle" left us with a "glorious heritage," while black people "have never created anything approximating a civilization." Slavery, he wrote, was "successfully defended from a Biblical standpoint" until "the institution's legitimacy was systematically undermined in the name of 'equality' and misappropriated 'Christian ethics.'"[15]

---

[10]The Knights Party website (8 November 2012). *America's White Future Begins Here.*
[11]MacLean, N. (2010). "Neo-Confederacy versus the New Deal: The Regional Utopia of the Modern American Right" in *The Myth of Southern Exceptionalism.* p. 309.
[12]See footnote 9.
[13]Potok, M. (Spring 2012). *The Year in Hate & Extremism.* Southern Poverty Law Center, Intelligence Report, Issue 145.
[14]*Ibid.*
[15]Southern Poverty Law Center. *Michael Hill.* Intelligence Files.

2.1.5 Neo-Nazis

Neo-Nazis are groups or individuals seeking to restore Nazism based on a modern National Socialism ideology. This ideology is founded on the legacy of the Nazi Third Reich and includes a veneration of Adolf Hitler and aggressive nationalism.[16] Neo-Nazism encompasses radical nationalism that furthers an agenda of anti-Semitism, homophobia, racism and xenophobia. Anti-Semitism is one of the foundational elements, and Holocaust denial is among those features intrinsic to the belief system. It is a global phenomenon with a presence in Asia, Europe and the Americas.

The American Nazi movement's historical beginnings can be traced to a nationalist organization identified as the German American Bund, which existed prior to World War II. The Nazi movement went underground until the formation of the American Nazi Party (ANP) in the United States.[17] Robert Brannon, member of the ANP before its decline, founded the National Socialist Movement (NSM) in 1974.[18] As early as 2004, the NSM dominated the national scene as a result of the internal disarray of the National Alliance (NA), which was founded by William Pierce, author of *The Turner Diaries*. Today, the NSM is self-described as the largest and most active National Socialist party in the United States.[19]

The NSM advocates violence circuitously, presumably to limit attention from federal law enforcement agencies and watchdog groups. NSM Commander Jeff Schoep's admonition on the group's website warns, "Acts of violence or terrorism against America or its Citizens is unacceptable and not tolerated within the ranks of the National Socialist Movement."[20] Nevertheless, they have been known to respond in uniform, armed, and with the intent to enforce the law or patrol the neighborhood streets. This was demonstrated in the 2011 counter-protest of the Occupy Phoenix demonstration[21] and also in response to the 2012 NBPP's bounty for the apprehension of George Zimmerman.[22]

---

[16]"Neo-Nazism" (2002). Faculty of Humanities at Charles University in Prague, Department of Civil Society Studies.

[17]Gods of the Third Reich website (23 February 2012*). Nazism: Still Alive in the USA.*

[18]*Ibid.*

[19]National Socialist Movement website.

[20]*Ibid.*

[21]Phoenix Class War Council (15 October 2011). *The National Socialist Movement Scum Show Up Armed to Counter Protest #Occupyphoenix.*

[22]Shahid, A. (7 April 2012). *Neo-Nazis Patrolling Streets of Sanford, Fla., Where Trayvon Shot and Killed.* New York Daily News.

2.1.6 White Power Skinheads

The original Skinhead subculture emerged in the 1960s, largely in Europe, and was not defined by race. It is important to note that initially, the Skinhead movement had no nexus with White nationalism or the neo-Nazi ideologies. As the movement spread across the world, however, one neo-Nazi Skinhead faction found a home in the United States.

In the 1990s, the racist skinhead movement picked up where more traditional groups (such as the KKK, neo-Nazis and the White Aryan Resistance) left off. Their philosophy was reminiscent of the message in the *Turner Diaries*—to engage in violent acts with the intent of igniting a U.S. race war. Employing the leaderless resistance strategy of Texan white nationalist Louis Beam, the long-term objective was to remove Jews, minorities, liberals and their white conspirators of the ZOG from power. Increasing in lethality since 9/11 and continuing to attack immigrants and desecrate synagogues, Skinheads have rejected their trademarked shaved head and steel-toed boots and adopted a more contemporary look.

Although the groups are not rooted in religion, they leveraged the 9/11 terror attacks to suit their ideological goals. They chose to emulate the successes of Islamic extremists, understanding the power of a movement based on religious fervor. This religious evolution gained considerable traction by the skinheads housed in America's prisons. Unfortunately, most often skinheads who are taken off the streets, prosecuted and convicted under strict hate crime statutes become a force multiplier once incarcerated. Being housed with their most violent colleagues facilitates unprecedented personal bonding, a new proving ground and unique opportunities. In addition to the race-based crimes inside and outside of prison, groups such as the Nazi Low Riders morphed into criminal enterprises, profiting in narcotics trafficking, identity theft, and murder.

The zeal for their religiosity is matched only in their engagement in their trademark hate music, which includes white power, heavy metal, Celtic and folk genres. The diversity of the Racist Skinhead movement presents a complex counterterrorism dilemma.

2.1.7 White Nationalists

This is a broad ideological category, including groups whose principles revolve around racially based hatred, white supremacy and/or white separatist ideologies. The roots of contemporary White Nationalism are traced to the NA, founded in Hillsboro, West Virginia, by university physics professor Dr. William Luther Pierce in 1974. As a former associate of George Lincoln Rockwell, the assassinated leader of the ANP, Pierce took advantage of group infighting and commandeered the largest faction, reorganizing it into the NA. They adopted the slogans, "Free Men Are Not Equal" and "Equal Men Are Not Free."

Anti-Semitism is a core element of the NA ideology, which also asserts: Jews rule America and control its news and mass media outlets; support of the State of Israel was the genesis of the 9/11 attacks; and Israel's Mossad intelligence agency initiated the 2001 anthrax attacks to facilitate the U.S. 2003 invasion of Iraq.[23] NA goals include creating a "white living space" (not unlike South Africa's apartheid), an Aryan-based society, a white racially autonomous government, an educational system that teaches these racial principals, and a racially based economic policy. Although some violent neo-Nazis and other reactionaries may have been inspired by the NA's message, no acts of terrorism or hate crimes have been directly linked to the original group.[24]

Another White Nationalist group was born in 1983 when Robert Jay Matthews founded The Order, also known as the Bruder Schweigen (German for "Brothers Keep Silent") or Silent Brotherhood. Their goal was to establish a homeland free of Jews and other non-whites to separate themselves from the ZOG. They believed the only way to achieve this objective was through revolution. Matthews led The Order into a counterfeiting operation, robberies and other crimes for the purpose of funding future operations. Eventually, the group bombed the Congregation Ahavath Israel Synagogue in Boise, Idaho.

The violence escalated to murder when Matthews directed the killing of Order member Walter Edward West, who was thought to have shared the groups' secret operations while drunk. The Order was also suspected in the murder of Jewish talk show host Alan Berg, targeting him not only because he was Jewish but also because he ridiculed The Order on air.[25]

---

[23]Pate, R. (2004). *The anthrax mystery: solved.* National Vanguard, Issue 122.
[24]Martin, G. (2011). *Terrorism and Homeland Security.* SAGE Publications, Thousand Oaks, CA.
[25]The Denver Post (18 June 2009). *The Murder of Alan Berg in Denver: 25 Years Later.*

In 1984, the FBI arrested Thomas Martinez, who became an informant. During the attempted arrest of Matthews, the group founder managed to escape to his bunker at Whidbey Island in Washington. This led to a 36-hour shootout with the FBI, where Matthews eventually died when the structure caught fire. News reports about the siege on Whidbey Island were the first time the American public learned about The Order and their war against the ZOG.[26]

2.2 RELIGIOUS IDEOLOGY

Violent motivations bleed across ideological lines, and racial and religious inspirations often work in concert to propel HVE. Recognizing the inherently messy ideological landscape, some of the religious motivations draw on radical interpretations of major world religions.

2.2.1 Christian Identity

The term "Christian Identity" has two distinct meanings.[27] Anglo-Israelism (also called British-Israelism) is a belief that the Anglo-Saxon, Celtic, Scandinavian, Germanic and associated cultures are the racial descendants of the tribes of Israel. Christian Identity also refers to racist, Christian-based faith groups. A number of small, ultraconservative Fundamentalist Christian denominations have accepted Anglo-Israelism and grafted it to racist, sexist, anti-communist, and homophobic beliefs. They also view the Jewish people as descendants of Satan.

In the context of North America, the latter definition has become dominant, associated with churches, religious organizations, extreme right-wing political groups, and in some instances, survivalists. Christian Identity adherents hold that "non-whites are soulless beasts also called the Mud People."[28] Dr. Michael Barkun, a leading expert on the Christian Identity movement, writes that "this virulent racist and anti-Semitic theology, which is practiced by over 50,000 people in the United States alone, is prevalent among many right wing extremist groups and has been called the 'glue' of the racist right."[29] Christian

---

[26]HistoryLink.org. *Robert Jay Mathews, Founder of the White-Supremacist Group The Order, Is Killed During an FBI Siege on Whidbey Island on December 8, 1984.*
[27]Religious Tolerance website. *Christian Identity Movement.*
[28]See footnote 24.
[29]Religious Tolerance website. *Christian Identity Movement.*

Identity is particularly dangerous because it presents hate as a religious duty and murder as an act of faith.[30]

The Christian Identity movement sits at the nexus of normally antagonistic segments of the far right, providing a vehicle to unite groups that were previously at odds. Christian Identity offered a way for varying groups to align crosscutting objectives, such as efforts against the ZOG.

Before the turn of the millennium, the FBI produced a report analyzing organizations that believed the year 2000 would bring the end of the world. The domestic terrorism report was entitled "Project Megiddo." The report presents Wesley A. Swift as the most significant figure in the early Christian Identity movement in the United States. A former Methodist minister, Swift founded the White Identity Church of Jesus Christ—Christian in the 1940s (later renamed the Church of Jesus Christ Christian).[31] Other Christian Identity churches have arisen, all preaching a similar belief that Aryans are a chosen race.[32]

Foundational Christian Identity objectives include preparation for the end of the world, in which the chosen group will play a fundamental role. The Megiddo Report states that "Christian Identity adherents ... believe they are among those chosen by God to wage this battle during Armageddon, and they will be the last line of defense for the white race and Christian America." Readying the group for this important role entails survivalist and paramilitary training, in addition to storing food, supplies, weapons, and ammunition.[33]

2.2.2 Aryan Nations

Richard Butler established the Aryan Nations as a "political counterpart to his Christian Identity sect, called the Church of Jesus Christ Christian."[34] The organization was originally based in Hayden Lake, Idaho, a 20-acre compound that served as headquarters, hosting the annual World Congress of Aryan Nations, attended by direct members and those of similar groups.[35] The meeting brought together Klansman

---

[30]Coulson, D.O. (2001) *No Heroes: Inside the FBI's Secret Counter-Terrorism Force.*
[31]FBI (20 October 1999). *Project Megiddo.* Christian Identity. Center for Studies on New Religions.
[32]*Ibid.*
[33]*Ibid.*
[34]See footnote 24.
[35]Anti-Defamation League. *Aryan Nations/Church of Jesus Christ Christian.*

from across the country, Posse Comitatus leaders, tax resisters, National Socialist groups, Christian Identity church delegations and other right-wing, unaffiliated individuals.[36] In 2001, FBI Director Louis Freeh identified Aryan Nations as a continuing terrorist threat,[37] and the RAND Corporation deemed them "the first truly nationwide terrorist network."[38]

2.2.3 The Creativity Movement

Ben Klassen founded the Creativity Movement (originally the World Church of the Creator), whose ideologies are influential in the Christian Identity movement. Klassen declared that the white race is doomed if it does not change course and avoid being overcome by people of color, described as crossbreeds. The Creativity Movement goes so far as to propose a rejection of Christianity, which some adherents believe was created as a Jewish conspiracy to enslave whites.[39]

Another Creativity Movement leader was Matthew Hale, identified as the church's supreme leader and Pontifex Maximus. The articulate, charismatic and handsome Hale leveraged every media opportunity, always cautious to skirt the issue of directly advocating violence. He routinely shared his messages of white supremacy and hate during television interviews. He was also one of the first ideological extremists to take advantage of the Internet, using it to recruit women and children with sites directly catering to those demographics. On April 6, 2005, Hale was sentenced to a 40-year prison term for soliciting an undercover FBI informant to kill federal judge Joan Lefkow, who was presiding over a copyright case regarding the name of his organization.[40]

2.2.4 Muslim Identity

Following the 9/11 terrorist attacks, Islam came to be viewed by many as somehow inherently violent. It is important to note that the

[36]Coates, J. (1987). *Armed and Dangerous: The Rise of the Survivalist Right*. Hill and Wang, New York, NY.

[37]FBI Congressional Statement (10 May 2001). *Statement for the Record, Louis J. Freeh, Director Federal Bureau of Investigation on the Threat of Terrorism to the United States Before the United States Senate Committees on Appropriations, Armed Services, and Select Committee on Intelligence.*

[38]START—National Consortium for the Study of Terrorism and Responses to Terrorism. *Aryan Nations (AN).*

[39]See footnote 24.

[40]Wilogren, J. (9 January 2003). *White Supremacist Is Held in Ordering Judge's Death.* New York Times.

overwhelming majority of the Muslim community is not joining or supporting factions of radical Islamic groups. Muslims around the world have rejected extremist movements and voice their opposition, sometimes at great risk of physical harm. Recognizing that people use a religious framework to justify violent activity (and not the other way around), "Muslim Identity" refers specifically to the individuals and the ideologies associated with HVE.

The organizing principle behind Muslim Identity is a worldview that there is a predatory relationship between "the West" (broadly, the United States and Europe) and the Islamic world (Muslim-majority nations). The perceived motivations for Western aggression include control of natural resources, as well as the destruction of Islam as a religious or political force.[41] Terrorism expert Peter Bergen, who interviewed Osama bin Laden, wrote that, "For bin Laden and his followers, the world is explained by the idea that Islam is under assault by the West, in particular the United States, and that only by attacking America will this state of affairs ever be reversed."[42]

Unlike other extremist groups discussed here, Muslim Identity adherents often do not belong to a cohesive group. The perceived West-versus-Islam dichotomy, however, does yield a unifying idea and common ideological basis. Central to this philosophical framework is the complex notion of jihad.

Jihad is fundamentally a religious duty, but its meaning and interpretation have been inconsistent across the centuries. The word conveys a "struggle," literally meaning "striving" or "determined effort."[43] There are two broad interpretations: the greater and lesser jihad.[44] The "greater jihad" is an internal struggle by the believer to fulfill their religious obligations. There is no violent element in this interpretation. The "lesser jihad" is the physical struggle against enemies of Islam.

Muslim Identity proponents focus almost exclusively on the lesser jihad.[45] What is more, their interpretation of the lesser jihad departs

[41]Ibish, H. (2010). *Muslim Extremism Stems from Alienation*. The Washington Post.
[42]Bergen, P.L. (2011). *The Longest War: The Enduring Conflict Between America and al Qaeda*.
[43]Streusand, D.E. (September 1997). *What does jihad mean?* The Middle East Quarterly, 4(3), 9–17.
[44]Morgan, D. (2010). *Essential Islam: A Comprehensive Guide to Belief and Practice*. Praeger, p. 87.
[45]See footnote 43.

significantly from historically traditional views, which held that the lesser jihad was only applicable when resisting an invading force that prohibited the free practice of Islam. For Muslim Identity adherents, the lesser jihad came to include offensive action in foreign lands with a much broader, vaguer notion of what constituted an invading force that threatened Islamic practice.

Offensive jihad found its most significant advocate in al Qaeda, whose escalating terror attacks against the United States, culminating on 9/11, captured worldwide attention and amplified the group's Muslim Identity ideology. The message that Islam was in peril in the face of Western hegemony cut across historical and sectarian lines, drawing membership from all strata of society. Ideologically, al Qaeda demonstrated a remarkable capacity to render Sunni-Shia differences irrelevant, focusing on western nations and their influence on regional regimes, viewed as apostate for their alliance with the United States and Europe, as well as their more secular method of rule.

In May 2007, in a profound demonstration of al Qaeda's capacity as an adaptive adversary, Ayman al-Zawahiri, al Qaeda's second-in-command, reached out to African-Americans. In an interview with Al Sahab Media, al-Zawahiri invoked speeches by Malcolm X, linking the idea of global jihad with the continued struggle of oppressed African Americans.[46]

Initial impressions concluded this was an ineffective tactic on a non-receptive audience; however, the creation of African-American Muslim extremist organizations before and since al-Zawahiri's outreach cannot be ignored. Homegrown groups such as Jam'iyyat Ul-Islam Is-Saheeh (JIS), the terror cell formed in a California State prison, and Jamaat ul-Fuqra (JF), a paramilitary organization of African-Americans based in Pakistan and the United States, have resonated with certain demographics, most of all inmates in the United States.

After the 1993 World Trade Center attack, JF was considered "perhaps the most dangerous fundamentalist sect operating in the United States."[47] Arabic for "community of the impoverished," JF was founded by Shaykh Mubarak Ali Gilani. United States and Pakistani intelligence

---

[46]Al Sahab Media (16 June 2007). *Interview with Shaykh Ayman al-Zawahiri.*
[47]Hosenball, M. (27 February 1994). *Another Holy War: Waged on American Soil.* Newsweek Magazine.

officials have accused JF of militant and criminal activities in the United States and abroad, including the murder of religious and ideological rivals on United States soil.[48] Prior to his abduction and eventual murder, American journalist Daniel Pearl was on his way to interview Gilani to investigate reports that shoe bomber Richard C. Reid studied under him in Lahore, Pakistan.[49]

Other U.S. citizen adherents to the Muslim Identity ideology engaged in the messaging efforts include:

- Adam Yahiya Gadahn (born Adam Perlman), also known as Azzam al-Amriki. He is a senior operative who has been a continued spokesperson and media advisor for al Qaeda since 2004. He is alleged to be hiding in Yemen.
- Omar Hammami (born Omar Shafik Hammami), also known as Abu Mansoor al-Amriki. He moved to Somalia in 2006, joining the al Qaeda affiliate al-Shabaab to become their media spokesperson, employing speeches and rap videos to draw potential recruits.
- Samir Khan, a Pakistani-American who grew up in New York. He became editor and publisher of *Inspire*, the English-language online magazine published by al Qaeda in the Arabian Peninsula (AQAP).
- Anwar al-Awlaki (born Anwar bin Nasser bin Abdulla al-Aulaqi) was an imam and senior al Qaeda recruiter with incredible influence. Al-Awlaki's ability to connect with a diverse population of adherents on several continents was profound. He was linked to a series of attacks and plots across the world and was killed along with Samir Khan by a U.S. drone strike in Yemen in 2011.

2.2.5 Jewish Defense League

While Christian and Muslim Identity groups constitute the majority of extremist groups operating in the United States, other groups following other religious beliefs have presented a domestic threat. The Jewish Defense League (JDL) espoused a variation of a Malcolm X mantra—protecting Jews from anti-Semitism "by any means necessary."[50] Founded in 1968 by Rabbi Meir Kahane, the Jewish militant group's expressed purpose (interestingly, much like the original

---

[48]Komerath, N. (2002). *Pakistani role in terrorism against the U.S.A.* Bharat Rakshak Monitor, 5(September–October).
[49]Zambelis, C. (11 August 2006). *Radical trends in African-American Islam*. Terrorism Monitor, 4(16).
[50]Anti-Defamation League. *About the Jewish Defense League*.

Black Panther Party at that time) was to mitigate the failed efforts of the U.S. government to safeguard American Jews. Kahane's oratory rhetoric mirrored Malcolm X's early racist, violent and political extremist overtones, engaged in a mission to create an environment of fear amongst non-Jews.

The group's objective was the protection of Jewish people by targeting facilities, organizations and people identified as enemies. The diversity of their domestic adversary list cannot be understated, as it included Arab and Soviet properties, neo-Nazis, people of Middle Eastern descent, African-Americans, and even other Jews. Early efforts primarily targeted Soviets, eventually expanding to diplomats of any nation that supported the United Nations' effort to present Zionism as on par with racism. There was no group beyond reproach, demonstrated by the JDL's occupation of the American Civil Liberties Union Atlanta offices in 1981 to protest their representation of neo-Nazis in court, assaulting NSM leader Harold Covington 1 year later as he arrived at a studio building to appear on NBC. Later that evening on the *Tomorrow* show, Covington said, "All Jews should be gassed."[51]

Internationally, the JDL opposed any efforts by the State of Israel that would grant Palestinian claims to land in the region. One of their most noteworthy incidents occurred in 1994, when JDL member Baruch Goldstein killed 29 Palestinian Muslims kneeling in prayer in a West Bank mosque. It is reported that the JDL website justified Goldstein's mass murder by stating, "Goldstein took a preventative measure against yet another Arab attack on Jews."[52]

The FBI designated the JDL as a "right-wing terrorist group"[53] and "a known violent extremist Jewish organization"[54] in 2001 and 2004, respectively. Despite mirroring other extremist organizations with a zero-tolerance policy against terrorism, violence, and other felonious acts,[55] the organization was active in plotting and executing several acts of domestic terrorism, predominantly bombings. In the wake of the 9/11 attacks, the JDL targeted locations in California, including

[51]Southern Poverty Law Center. *Jewish Defense League.*
[52]*Ibid.*
[53]FBI website. *Terrorism 2000/2001.* Reports and Publications.
[54]Statement of John Pistole before the *National Commission on Terrorist Attacks upon the United States* (14 April 2004).
[55]Several sources make note of this disclaimer, quoting a JDL website that is no longer online.

the King Fahd Mosque in Culver City, the Muslim Public Affairs Council in Los Angeles, and the San Clemente office of Congressman Darrell Issa, who is of Lebanese descent. JDL leader Irv Rubin and JDL member Earl Krugel were arrested for the plot. Taped conversations of Krugel included a statement that the attacks would serve as "a wakeup call" to Arabs.[56] Rubin allegedly committed suicide in prison under unusual circumstances—slitting his throat *before* jumping out of a window. Unknown assailants later killed Krugel in prison.

2.2.6 Aum Shinrikyo

Another telling example of religiously motivated extremism is Aum Shinrikyo, a Japanese religious cult that evolved into a violent extremist, anti-government movement. Shoko Asahara, a legally blind former yoga instructor, originally seeking to organize and develop the group using the government's guidelines for religious organizations, founded Aum Shinrikyo in 1984. In addition to tax breaks, organizations in Japan granted "religious group" status were exempted from future government investigations regarding their ideology or activities.

The importance of charismatic leadership was not wasted on Asahara, who declared himself "Christ" and a fully enlightened master of an ideology based on a variety of Eastern and Western mystic religious beliefs, including the works of sixteenth century French astronomer Nostradamus.[57] Emblematic of extremist organizations, he recruited adherents by prophesizing a doomsday scenario, accompanied by conspiracies associated with the British Royal Family, the Dutch, Freemasons, Jews and competing groups.[58] Under the cover of religion, the cult grew in size and scope from 10,000 members in 1992 to approximately 50,000 worldwide in 1995, with a presence in 6 countries and a net worth of more than $1 billion.[59]

In 1990, 25 Aum Shinrikyo members, including Asahara, were defeated in an election bid for parliament. This was a tipping point for the group, fueling conspiratorial government rhetoric and further

[56]Bohn, M.K. (2004). *The Achille Lauro Hijacking: Lessons in the Politics and Prejudice of Terrorism.* pp. 176–177.
[57]Snow, R.L. (2003). *Deadly Cults: The Crimes of True Believers.* p. 17.
[58]Goldwag, A. (2009). *Cults, Conspiracies, and Secret Societies: The Straight Scoop on Freemasons, the Illuminati, Skull and Bones, Black Helicopters, the New World Order, and Many, Many More.* Random House, p. 15.
[59]Senate Government Affairs Permanent Subcommittee on Investigations (31 October 1995). *Global Proliferation of Weapons of Mass Destruction: A Case Study on the Aum Shinrikyo.*

isolating the group from societal interaction. It drove recruitment activity and lethal (albeit innovative) plans for attacks on the Japanese population. Biological agents became Aum Shinrikyo's signature.

The group initially sought to aerosolize anthrax to create an inhalation anthrax epidemic. Reminiscent of other extremist groups bent on doomsday scenarios, they believed this would trigger a global war, positioning Asahara to ascend as the leader of the world. The first attack occurred in Matsumoto (1994) surrounding a real estate lawsuit involving Aum Shinrikyo. Choosing to deploy sarin, a deadly nerve agent, the group used a converted refrigerator truck as a delivery platform to disperse a cloud of sarin near the homes of the presiding judges who were likely to rule against Aum Shinrikyo. The attack killed seven and injured more than 500 people.[60]

Continuing their focus on the government, specifically the Japanese police department, Aum Shinrikyo set their sights on the Tokyo districts of Kasumigaseki and Nagatacho, home to the country's government offices, including the Prime Minister's residence. On March 20, 1995, 10 Aum Shinrikyo adherents launched a coordinated, simultaneous multi-pronged attack, releasing sarin on five trains in the Tokyo subway system. The attack killed 12 people and injured almost 3,800 more.[61]

Although the 1995 attack was the most deadly, the group's research and development efforts spanned the globe, including forays into West Africa in an attempt to weaponize the Ebola virus, as well as experimentation with a variety of biological agent dispersal methods in and around Tokyo. Aum Shinrikyo is a perfect example of a violent extremist organization that possessed the necessary ingredients for terrorist action: *alienated individuals* inspired by a charismatic leader, following a *legitimizing ideology* that targeted the government, with the encouragement of an *enabling environment*, the supportive familial structure of Aum itself.

2.3 ISSUE-ORIENTED IDEOLOGY

This category includes a number of groups and ideologies targeting a range of constructs (including the U.S. government) driven by specific grievances and single-issue priorities. As with race and religion, the

---

[60]CDC website, Centers for Disease Control. *Aum Shinrikyo: Once and Future Threat?*
[61]*Ibid.*

issue-oriented category is often crosscutting, touching on more than one legitimizing ideology.

2.3.1 Anti-government

Sovereign Citizen is a loosely affiliated group and ideology based on conspiratorial beliefs regarding the legitimacy of the founding of the United States. The premise, called "Redemption Theory," claims the U.S. government went bankrupt when it abandoned the gold standard in 1933.[62] The theory proposes the existence of direct accounts in the Treasury Department that belong to "straw men" acting in the name of unsuspecting people as part of a currency conspiracy.

The Sovereign Citizen ideology posits that adherents are not subject to the local, state, or federal laws of the United States and may refuse to recognize the authority of the courts. Some followers even believe they can use armed force to resist police arrest.[63] A 2011 FBI bulletin notes that since 2000, lone-offender Sovereign Citizen extremists have killed six law enforcement officers. Timothy McVeigh's co-conspirator in the Oklahoma City bombing, Terry Nichols, was a Sovereign Citizen[64] and both men had attended Michigan Militia meetings.[65] Sovereign citizens do not represent an anarchist group, nor are they necessarily a militia, although they sometimes use or buy illegal weapons.[66]

A number of issues regarding the threat potential for this group concern the escalation to violence and the lack of a geographic or demographic profile. The FBI has said that the Sovereign Citizen ideology "intrinsically deals with the rejection, complete rejection, of the constitutional authority of the United States or any other government for that matter ... that when you have an encounter with law enforcement, we have seen that has a potential to go high and right very fast." Amplifying the threat is the challenge of discerning membership

[62]U.S. Department of Justice, Federal Bureau of Investigation, Domestic Terrorism Operations Unit II (2010). *Sovereign Citizens: An Introduction for Law Enforcement.*
[63]Bennett, Brian (23 February 2012). *"Sovereign Citizen" Movement Now on FBI's Radar.* Los Angeles Times.
[64]Schendel, S. *Since 2000, Lone-Offender Sovereign-Citizen Extremists Have Killed Six Law Enforcement Officers.* Murrow News Service.
[65]D'Oro, R. (20 November 2009). *Militia Movement Resurfaces Across Nation.* Associated Press.
[66]FBI website (2011). *Sovereign Citizens: A Growing Domestic Threat to Law Enforcement.* FBI Counterterrorism Analysis Section.

and location, inasmuch as Sovereign Citizens are not localized in any one part of the country and vary by age, gender, and race.[67]

The political resistance strategy of Sovereign Citizens is reminiscent of Louis Beam's "leaderless resistance" or covert cell structure and is considered the first important advocate for this strategy.[68] Leaderless resistance followers may engage a variety of actions, including nonviolent disruption and civil disobedience, as well as acts of terror, such as bombings and targeted assassinations. This arrangement allows adherents to operate autonomously, lacking a formal hierarchical command and control structure, and only gathering in groups as necessary to train and share ideology.

Sovereign Citizens adhere to a concept that the county sheriff is the highest legitimate law enforcement officer in the land. Daniel Levitas, author of *The Terrorist Next Door*, a book that chronicles the racist underpinnings of the militia movements of the 1990s, writes that "ever since the notion of the supremacy of the county sheriff became popularized, it has continued to remain attractive – although when people hear it they don't understand that what is behind it is violent lawlessness and vigilantism."[69]

Also under the antigovernment umbrella is the Patriot social movement, which is characterized as independent, conservative, and may consist of individual or combinations of several groups, such as Christian Identity, tax protesters, Sovereign Citizens, militia members and others. The ideology espouses that American liberties are in jeopardy and that elected officials (as well as the government itself) is illegitimate.

The 1992 Ruby Ridge standoff in northern Idaho and the 1993 siege of the Branch Davidian compound in Waco, Texas, were rallying events for the Patriot movement. Following these events, the Patriot and Militia movements became active in all 50 states, with numbers increasing significantly – between 20,000 and 60,000 adherents.[70] Activity waned during the George W. Bush administration, but since the election of President

---

[67]Sullivan, E. (6 February 2012). *Sovereign Citizens Are Extremists Watched By FBI*. Huffington Post.

[68]Laqueur, W. (2000). *The New Terrorism: Fanaticism and the Arms of Mass Destruction*. Oxford University Press, p. 110.

[69]Lenz, R. (2012). *Resurrection*. Intelligence Report. Winter 2012, Issue 148, p. 18.

[70]Berlet, C. and Lyons, M. (2000). *Right Wing Populism in America: Too Close for Comfort*.

Obama, the number of Patriot and militia organizations in the United States has swelled to 1,274, nearly 10 times that under President Bush.[71]

2.3.2 Anti-abortion

Anti-abortion violence as it relates to HVE is somewhat unique to the United States, and related incidents have been notably absent from government terrorism databases. This may be attributed to two ongoing concerns: the continuing debate over the definition of terrorism; and the often partisan debate challenging the "politically motivated violence" being advanced during these attacks. The consternation over the nexus between anti-abortion attacks and terrorism was exacerbated in the 1980s when, despite documented patterns of escalating violence, FBI Director William Webster declared that the spate of clinic bombings and attacks by anti-abortionists did not conform to the federal definition of terrorism and therefore was not a priority for federal investigation.[72]

Inasmuch as race or issue-oriented motivations are often drivers associated with anti-abortion extremist violence, it would suggest these incidents meet the HVE threshold. Additionally, the political objectives associated with violence meant to influence legislation that limits or prohibits choice or access to appropriate medical care certainly seems to meet the parameters of the definition of terrorism used here.

The Army of God (AOG) is the best example of the escalating extremist activities associated with anti-abortion groups. Don Benny Anderson first mentioned AOG when he, along with Matthew and Wayne Moore, kidnapped an Illinois abortion provider and his wife. Ultimately, the couple was released unharmed, though the three were previously responsible for abortion clinic arsons.[73] Beginning in 1982, the AOG launched a series of bombings and arson attacks on clinics in Florida,[74] Virginia, and Washington, DC, as well as issued a death threat to Supreme Court Justice Harry Blackmun, a Republican and the author of the *Roe v. Wade* opinion.[75]

[71]Memmott, M. (8 March 2012). *Report: "Explosive" Growth Of "Patriot Movement" and Militias Continues.* NPR.
[72]Kushner, H. (2003). *Encyclopedia of Terrorism.* Sage Publications, Thousand Oaks, CA, pp. 38–39.
[73]National Abortion Federation website. *Anti-Abortion Extremists: The Army of God and Justifiable Homicide.*
[74]Kushner. *Encyclopedia of Terrorism.* p. 38.
[75]Yarbrough, T. (2008). *Harry A. Blackmun: The Outsider Justice.* Oxford University Press, New York, NY, p. 281.

In 1993, Rachelle Ranae "Shelley" Shannon, an anti-abortion activist, shot Dr. George Tiller in both arms outside his abortion clinic in Wichita, Kansas.[76] The AOG website describes Shannon as a "soldier" and "part of Operation Rescue," responsible for 35 different violent anti-abortion actions.[77] She later blew up an abortion clinic, causing $175,000 in damage and forcing the clinic to relocate. She also sent a letter to *Life Advocate* magazine, in which she likened destruction and casualties to collateral damage, characterizing the attacks as war.[78]

2.3.3 Environmentalists

There are several groups that claim to be champions of single-issue causes. Single-issue extremists, such as the Animal Liberation Front (ALF) and Earth Liberation Front (ELF), have escalated their rhetoric and tactics and are becoming progressively more dangerous in their potential for violence. During 2002 congressional testimony, the FBI stated that "special interest extremism," such as the ALF and ELF, is a "serious terrorist threat."[79]

Acts committed in furtherance of their mission are also known as Eco-terrorism or ecotage, and the adherents are sometimes referred to as Eco-terrorists or "ecoteurs." As is common with previously mentioned groups, ALF and ELF often share members and may coordinate their activities. The ALF mission is "to effectively allocate resources (time and money) to end the 'property' status of nonhuman animals."[80] ALF argues that subjecting animals to property status is "speciesism,"[81] a term coined by Richard Ryder, British writer and psychologist, to describe the exclusion of nonhuman animals from the protections available to human beings.

Using a leaderless resistance cell structure, ALF has a presence in more than 40 countries,[82] and although engaging in terrorist tactics resulting in property damage, they maintain a strict code of not

---

[76]Philips, D. (22 August 1993). *Violence Hardly Ruffled Protest Ritual*. The Washington Post.
[77]Army of God website. *Who is Shelley Shannon?*
[78]*Ibid.*
[79]FBI Congressional Testimony (12 February 2002). *Testimony of James F. Jarboe, Domestic Terrorism Section Chief, Counterterrorism Division, FBI, Before the House Resources Committee, Subcommittee on Forests and Forest Health, "The Threat of Eco-Terrorism."*
[80]Animal Liberation Front website. *About ALF, Mission Statement.*
[81]Ryder, R.D. (2009). Speciesism. In Marc Bekoff (Ed.), *Encyclopedia of Animal Rights and Animal Welfare.* p. 320
[82]Bite Back (2011). *Diary of Actions.*

harming people.[83] They have published their activities via the magazine *Bite Back,* which describes itself as "dedicated to the advocacy of those caught or currently in the underground for animal liberation." In 2004, *Direct Action Report* claimed that "17,262 animals were 'liberated' and 554 acts of sabotage, vandalism and arson were carried out."[84]

The origin of the ELF is unclear. Their relationship with ALF, however, as described by the Animal Liberation Press Office, declares the groups share a common approach of using direct action to interrupt those profiting (and in their words, "plundering") the natural environment. Both organizations are organized into cells known only to their members.[85]

The numerous extremist groups organized under racial, religious and issue-oriented ideologies present serious concerns for countering HVE. Yet, while ideologies are a critical component of violent extremism, they do not on their own create terrorists. Indeed, while there are tens of thousands of Americans actively involved with the above-mentioned groups, a comparatively small number of their members use violence to further their ideological goals. The reason some extremists turn violent while others do not is best investigated through an analysis of the radicalization pathway.

FURTHER READING

Ali, A.Y. (2009). *The Meaning of the Holy Qur'an* (11th ed.). Amana Publications, Beltsville, MD.

Al Sahab Media (16 June 2007). *Interview with Shaykh Ayman al-Zawahiri.* YouTube. http://www.youtube.com/watch?v = haWoMdmgwws (Retrieved: 28 December 2012).

American Civil Liberties Union. *Arizona's SB 1070.* http://www.aclu.org/arizonas-sb-1070 (Retrieved: 30 December 2012).

American Resistance Movement website. (2012). http://americanmilitiamovement.com/Retrieved (Retrieved: 29 December 2012).

Anderson, K. (19 November 2002). *US Muslims Suffer Backlash.* BBC News. http://news.bbc.co.uk/2/hi/americas/2488829.stm (Retrieved: 23 December 2012).

Animal Liberation Front website. *About ALF, Mission Statement.* http://www.animalliberation-front.com/ALFront/mission_statement.htm (Retrieved: 2 January 2013).

Anti-Defamation League. *Extremism in America, American Front.* http://www.adl.org/learn/ext_us/american_front/default.asp?LEARN_Cat = Extremism&LEARN_SubCat = Extremism_in_America&xpicked = 3&item = american_front (Retrieved: 16 December 2012).

[83]Blejwas, A., Griggs, A., and Potok, M. (2005). *Terror from the Right Almost 60 Terrorist Plots Uncovered in the U.S.*
[84]Anti-Defamation League. *Radical Animal Rights Magazine Issues 2004 "Direct Action" Report.*
[85]North American Animal Liberation Front Press Office. *Frequently Asked Questions About the North American Animal Liberation Press Office.*

Anti-Defamation League (1996). *Farrakhan in His Own Words—On Homosexuals.* Kansas City speech. http://www.adl.org/special_reports/farrakhan_own_words2/on_homosexuals. asp (Retrieved: 24 November 2012).

Anti-Defamation League. *About the Jewish Defense League.* http://archive.adl.org/extremism/ jdl_chron.asp (Retrieved: 22 May 2013).

Anti-Defamation League. *Neo-Nazi Skinheads and Racist Rock: Youth Subculture of Hate.* http:// www.adl.org/poisoning_web/racist_rock.asp (Retrieved: 16 December 2012).

Anti-Defamation League. *Aryan Nations/Church of Jesus Christ Christian.* http://www.webcitation.org/5 × 8bud3Xk (Retrieved: 21 December 2012).

Anti-Defamation League. *Radical Animal Rights Magazine Issues 2004 "Direct Action" Report.* http://www.adl.org/learn/extremism_in_america_updates/movements/ecoterrorism/eco050125.htm (Retrieved: 2 January 2013).

Archibold, R.C. (24 April 2010). *Arizona Enacts Stringent Law on Immigration.* The New York Times. http://www.nytimes.com/2010/04/24/us/politics/24immig.html?ref = us&_r = 0 (Retrieved: 30 December 2012).

Army of God website. *Who is Shelley Shannon?* http://www.armyofgod.com/ShelleyWhois.html (Retrieved: 1 January 2013).

Associated Press (22 May 2002). *Militia Members Guilty in Bomb Plot.* http://www.rickross.com/ reference/militia/militia73.html (Retrieved: 29 December 2012).

Associated Press (28 October 2008). *Obama Plot Arrests Shock Suspects' Neighbors Neo-Nazis Allegedly Planned School Massacre Before Targeting Democrat.* NBCNEWS.com. http://www. msnbc.msn.com/id/27416974/t/obama-plot-arrests-shock-suspects-neighbors/#.UM6SQY5y5US (Retrieved: 16 December 2012).

Baram, M. (4 January 2007). *White Supremacist Busted on Child-Porn Charge.* ABC News. http://abcnews.go.com/US/story?id = 2774119&page = 1#.UNEwho5y5UQ (Retrieved: 18 December 2012).

Barkun, M. (1997). *Religion and the Racist Right.* The University of North Carolina Press, Chapel Hill, NC.

BBC News (12 January 2010). *Islam4UK Islamist Group Banned Under Terror Laws.* http://news. bbc.co.uk/2/hi/uk_news/8453560.stm (Retrieved: 25 December 2012).

BBC News (30 September 2011). *Islamist Cleric Anwar al-Awlaki Killed in Yemen.* http://www. bbc.co.uk/news/world-middle-east-15121879 (Retrieved: 28 December 2012).

Beasley, D. (13 September 2012). *Ku Klux Klan Sues Georgia After Bid to "Adopt" Road Is Denied.* Reuters. http://www.reuters.com/article/2012/09/13/us-usa-georgia-kkk-idUSBRE88C1LY20120913? feedType = RSS&feedName = domesticNews (Retrieved: 9 December 2012).

Beirich, H. (2012). *The Year in Nativism.* Intelligence Report. Spring 2012, Issue 145.

Beirich, H. and Potok, M. (2009). The Nativist Lobby: Three Faces of Intolerance. Southern Poverty Law Center, Montgomery, AL.

Bennett, B. (23 February 2012). *"Sovereign citizen" Movement Now on FBI's Radar.* Los Angeles Times. http://articles.latimes.com/2012/feb/23/nation/la-na-terror-cop-killers-20120224 (Retrieved: 26 December 2012).

Bergen, P., Rowland, J. (11 September 2012). *11 Years After 9/11: Who Are the Terrorists?* CNN Opinion. http://www.cnn.com/2012/09/11/opinion/bergen-terror-september-11/index.html (Retrieved: 22 November 2012).

Bergen, P.L. (2011). *The Longest War: The Enduring Conflict Between America and al Qaeda.* Free Press, New York, NY.

Bergen, P.L. (2006). *The Osama bin Laden I Know.* Free Press, New York, NY.

Berlet, C. and Lyons, M. (2000). *Right Wing Populism in America: Too Close for Comfort*. The Guilford Press.

Best, S. and Nocella, A.J. (2006). *Igniting a Revolution: Voices in Defense of the Earth*. AK Press.

Bierbauer, C. (17 October 1995). *Million Man March: Its Goal More Widely Accepted Than It Leader*. CNN—U.S. News. http://www.cnn.com/US/9510/megamarch/10-17/notebook/ (Retrieved: 24 November 2012).

Bite Back (2011). *Diary of Actions*. http://www.directaction.info/news.htm (Retrieved: 2 January 2013).

Blejwas, A., Griggs, A., Potok, M. (2005). *Terror from the Right Almost 60 Terrorist Plots Uncovered in the U.S.* Intelligence Report. http://web.archive.org/web/20080506183458/www.splcenter.org/intel/intelreport/article.jsp?aid = 549.

Bohn, M.K. (2004). *The Achille Lauro Hijacking: Lessons in the Politics and Prejudice of Terrorism*. Potomac Books, Inc.

Borum, R. (2011). *Radicalization into violent extremism I: a review of social science theories*. Journal of Strategic Security, 4(4), 7–36.

Burnett, D. (2002). *Clash of Worlds: What Christians Can Do in a World of Cultures in Conflict*. Monarch Books, UK.

Center for American Progress—Think Progress (19 April 2012). *CHART: 17 Years After Oklahoma City Bombing, Right-Wing Extremism Is Significant Domestic Terror Threat*. http://thinkprogress.org/security/2012/04/19/467384/chart-right-wing-extremism-terror-threat-oklahoma-city/ (Retrieved: 22 November 2012).

CDC website, Centers for Disease Control. *Aum Shinrikyo: Once and Future Threat?* Kyle B. Olson, Research Planning, Inc., Arlington, Virginia.

CNN (2 November 2011). *Militia Members Plotted to Kill Federal Officials, Prosecutors Say*. http://www.cnn.com/2011/11/01/justice/georgia-militia-arrests/index.html (Retrieved: 29 December 2012).

Coates, J. (1987). *Armed and Dangerous: The Rise of the Survivalist Right*. Hill and Wang, New York. NY.

Coulson, D.O. (2001). *No Heroes: Inside the FBI's Secret Counter-Terrorism Force*. Simon & Schuster.

Davis, M. (26 March 2011). *Louis Farrakhan: U.S. Lacks Moral Authority to Attack Gadhafi*. Chicago Sun Times. http://www.suntimes.com/news/nation/4517685-418/louis-farrakhan-u.s.-lacks-moral-authority-to-attack-gadhafi (Retrieved: 25 November 2012).

Dees, M. and Corcoran, J. (1997). *Gathering Storm: America's Militia Threat*. Harper Collins, New York, NY.

Democracy Now (24 April 2009). *Rise of Right-Wing Extremism Linked to Recession*. http://www.democracynow.org/2009/4/24/rise_of_right_wing_extremism_linked   (Retrieved: 22 November 2012).

DeParle, J. (17 April 2011). *The Anti-Immigration Crusader*. The New York Times. http://www.nytimes.com/2011/04/17/us/17immig.html?pagewanted = all&_r = 0   (Retrieved: 31   December 2012).

Dobratz, B.A. (1997). *"White Power, White Pride!": The White Separatist Movement in the United States*. Twayne Publishers, London.

D'Oro, R. (20 November 2009). *Militia Movement Resurfaces Across Nation*. Associated Press. http://www.msnbc.msn.com/id/34070149/ns/us_news-life/t/militia-movement-resurfaces-across-nation/#.UOCnno5y5UQ (Retrieved: 30 December 2012).

Earth Liberation Front website. http://earth-liberation-front.org/ (Retrieved: 4 January 2013).

Ellison, J. (29 August 2012). *FEAR Plot to Overthrow U.S. Government Part of Rising Domestic Extremism.* The Daily Beast. http://www.thedailybeast.com/articles/2012/08/29/fear-plot-to-over-throw-u-s-government-part-of-rising-domestic-extremism.html (Retrieved: 22 November 2012).

Emerson, S. (2006). *Jihad Incorporated: A Guide to Militant Islam in the US.* Prometheus Books, Amherst, NY.

Experts123 website. *Q: Does the League of the South Advocate Political Violence, Law Breaking, or Civil Disobedience as a Means of Accomplishing Our Objectives?* Note: response redirected to the Texas League of the South website. http://www.experts123.com/q/does-the-league-of-the-south-advocate-political-violence-law-breaking-or-civil-disobedience-as-a-means-of-accomplishing-our-objectives.html (Retrieved: 9 December 2012).

Extremist Groups: Information for Students (2006). *Army of God.* http://www.highbeam.com/doc/1G2-3447100033.html (Retrieved: 1 January 2013).

Falk, A. (5 December 2012). *Allgier Gets Life Without Parole for Killing Utah Corrections Officer.* The Salt Lake Tribune. http://www.sltrib.com/sltrib/mobile/55401821-68/allgier-anderson-fullerton-gun.html.csp (Retrieved: 16 December 2012).

Farrow, C. (4 February 2004). *Five White Men Face Charges in 2001 Attack.* Stormfront website. http://www.stormfront.org/forum/t114562/ (Retrieved: 16 December 2012).

FBI Congressional Statement (10 May 2001). *Statement for the Record, Louis J. Freeh, Director Federal Bureau of Investigation on the Threat of Terrorism to the United States Before the United States Senate Committees on Appropriations, Armed Services, and Select Committee on Intelligence.* http://web.archive.org/web/20010812035823/http://www.fbi.gov/congress/congress01/freeh051001.htm (Retrieved: 21 December 2012).

FBI Congressional Testimony (12 February 2002). *Testimony of James F. Jarboe, Domestic Terrorism Section Chief, Counterterrorism Division, FBI, Before the House Resources Committee, Subcommittee on Forests and Forest Health, "The Threat of Eco-Terrorism."* http://www2.fbi.gov/congress/congress02/jarboe021202.htm (Retrieved: 4 January 2013).

FBI website (6 February 2002). *Dale L. Watson, FBI Executive Assistant Director, Counterterrorism/Counterintelligence Division Testimony Before the Senate Select Committee on Intelligence, Washington, DC.* http://www.fbi.gov/news/testimony/the-terrorist-threat-confronting-the-united-states (Retrieved: 18 December 2012).

FBI website (16 February 2005). *Robert S. Mueller, III, Director, Federal Bureau of Investigation Testimony Before the Senate Committee on Intelligence of the United States, Washington, DC.* http://www.fbi.gov/news/testimony/global-threats-to-the-u.s.-and-the-fbis-response-1 (Retrieved: 25 December 2012).

FBI website (2011). *Sovereign Citizens: A Growing Domestic Threat to Law Enforcement.* FBI Counterterrorism Analysis Section. http://www.fbi.gov/stats-services/publications/law-enforce-ment-bulletin/september-2011/sovereign-citizens (Retrieved: 26 December 2012).

FBI website. *Eco-Terrorist Surrenders.* http://www.fbi.gov/news/news_blog/eco-terrorist-surrenders (Retrieved: 4 January 2013).

FBI website. *Terrorism 2000/2001.* Reports and Publications. http://www.fbi.gov/stats-services/publications/terror/terrorism-2000-2001/?searchterm = JDL (Retrieved: 24 May 2013).

FBI (20 October 1999). *Project Megiddo.* Christian Identity. Center for Studies on New Religions. http://www.cesnur.org/testi/FBI_006.htm (Retrieved: 20 December 2012).

Ford, P. (19 September 2001). *Europe cringes at Bush "Crusade" Against Terrorists.* The Christian Science Monitor. http://www.csmonitor.com/2001/0919/p12s2-woeu.html (Retrieved: 24 December 2012).

Gardell, M. (2003). *Gods of the Blood: The Pagan Revival and White Separatism.* Duke University Press Books, p. 69.

Gellman, B. (30 September 2010). *The Secret World of Extreme Militias.* Time Magazine. www.time.com/time/magazine/article/0,9171,2022636,00.html.

Gods of the Third Reich website (23 February 2012). *Nazism: Still Alive in the USA.* http://godsofthethirdreich.blogspot.com/2012_02_01_archive.html (Retrieved: 15 December 2012).

Goldwag, A. (2009). *Cults, Conspiracies, and Secret Societies: The Straight Scoop on Freemasons, the Illuminati, Skull and Bones, Black Helicopters, the New World Order, and Many, Many More.* Random House.

Gonzales, S. (19 February 2010). *Plane Crash Suspect's Home Mostly Destroyed by Fire.* Austin American-Statesman. http://www.statesman.com/news/news/local/plane-crash-suspects-home-mostly-destroyed-by-fi-1/nRqdm/ (Retrieved: 26 December 2012).

Goodrick-Clarke, N. (2003). *Black Sun: Aryan Cults, Esoteric Nazism, and the Politics of Identity.* NYU Press.

Gunaratna, R. (2003). *Inside al Qaeda, Global Network of Terror.* Berkley Publishing Group, New York, NY.

Hallowell, B. (16 April 2012). *Farrakhan Warns Young Leaders They Risk Being Killed If They Sell Out.* The Blaze. http://www.theblaze.com/stories/farrakhan-warns-young-leaders-they-risk-being-killed-if-they-sell-out/ (Retrieved: 25 November 2012).

Harnden, T. (3 August 2009). *Barack Obama Faces 30 Death Threats a Day, Stretching US Secret Service.* The Telegraph. http://www.telegraph.co.uk/news/worldnews/barackobama/5967942/Barack-Obama-faces-30-death-threats-a-day-stretching-US-Secret-Service.html (Retrieved: 9 December 2012).

Hastings, D. (23 February 1997). *Elohim City on Extremists' Underground Railroad.* Los Angeles Times. http://articles.latimes.com/1997-02-23/news/mn-31595_1_elohim-city (Retrieved: 22 December 2012).

Heim, J. (7 August 2012). *Wade Michael Page Was Steeped in neo-Nazi "Hate Music" Movement.* The Washington Post. http://articles.washingtonpost.com/2012-08-07/lifestyle/35493270_1_end-apathy-white-supremacist-mark-pitcavage (Retrieved: 16 December 2012).

Hernandez, A.R. (24 March 2012). *Trayvon Martin: New Black Panthers Offer $10,000 Bounty for Capture of Shooter George Zimmerman.* Orlando Sentinel. http://articles.orlandosentinel.com/2012-03-24/news/os-trayvon-martin-new-black-panthers-protest-20120324_1_sanford-vigilante-justice-black-men (Retrieved: 25 November 2012).

HistoryLink.org. *Robert Jay Mathews, Founder of the White-Supremacist Group The Order, Is Killed During an FBI Siege on Whidbey Island on December 8, 1984.* http://www.historylink.org/index.cfm?DisplayPage = output.cfm&file_id = 7921 (Retrieved: 19 December 2012).

Hosenball, M. (27 February 1994). *Another Holy War, Waged on American Soil.* Newsweek Magazine. http://www.thedailybeast.com/newsweek/1994/02/27/another-holy-war-waged-on-american-soil.html (Retrieved: 28 December 2012).

Huffpost Miami (9 May 2012). *Ten Alleged Members of American Front White Supremacist Group Arrested in Osceola County.* http://www.huffingtonpost.com/2012/05/08/american-front-osceola-county-arrested_n_1500296.html (Retrieved: 16 December 2012).

Huffington Post (20 April 2010). *Joe Stack STATEMENT: Alleged Suicide Note from Austin Pilot Posted Online.* http://www.huffingtonpost.com/2010/02/18/joe-stack-statement-alleg_n_467539.html (Retrieved: 26 December 2012).

Huffington Post (2012). *Abu Mansur Al Amriki, U.S. Jihadi in Somalia, Reportedly Claims Comrades Want to Kill Him (VIDEO).* http://www.huffingtonpost.com/2012/03/17/abu-mansur-al-amriki-video_n_1355387.html (Retrieved: 28 December 2012).

Huffington Post (12 November 2012). *Neo Nazi Immigration Protest Met with Clown Counter-Protest.* http://www.huffingtonpost.com/2012/11/12/neo-nazi-protest-immigration-clown_n_2118945.html (Retrieved: 30 December 2012.

Intelligence Report (2012). *The Year in Hate and Extremism: The "Patriot" Movement Explodes.* The Southern Poverty Law Center. Spring 2012/Issue 145.

Irwin, R. (31 October 2001). *Is This the Man Who Inspired Bin Laden?* The Guardian. http://www.guardian.co.uk/world/2001/nov/01/afghanistan.terrorism3 (Retrieved: 24 December 2012).

JIS Tutorial Protocol (14 December 2007). Case 8:05-cr-00214-CJC, Document 259-2. p. 16.

Kaleem, J. (29 February 2012). *Islam in America: Mosques See Dramatic Increase in Just Over a Decade, According to Muslim Survey.* Huffington Post. http://www.huffingtonpost.com/2012/02/29/mosques-in-united-states-study_n_1307851.html (Retrieved: 25 December 2012).

Kelleher, J.B. (8 August 2012). *Three Hutaree Militia Members Sentenced in Detroit to Time Served.* Reuters. http://www.reuters.com/article/2012/08/08/us-usa-security-hutaree-idUSBRE8770ZQ2012080 (Retrieved: 29 December 2012).

Komerath, N. (2002). Pakistani role in terrorism against the U.S.A.. Bharat Rakshak Monitor, 5 (September–October).

Krikorian, G., Moore, S. (1 September 2005). *4 Men Indicted in Alleged Plot to Spread Terror in the Southland.* LA Times.

Kushner, H. (2003). *Encyclopedia of Terrorism.* Sage Publications, Thousand Oaks, CA.

Laqueur, W. (2000). *The New Terrorism: Fanaticism and the Arms of Mass Destruction.* Oxford University Press.

League of the South website (9 December 2012). *On Secession and Southern Independence.* http://dixienet.org/rights/index.shtml (Retrieved: 9 December 2012).

League of the South website (9 December 2012). The *Right of Secession and Benefits of Independence for the South.* http://dixienet.org/rights/index.shtml (Retrieved: 9 December 2012).

Leiken, R.S., Brooke, S. (March/April 2007). *The Moderate Muslim Brotherhood.* Foreign Affairs. http://www.foreignaffairs.com/articles/62453/robert-s-leiken-and-steven-brooke/the-moderate-muslim-brotherhood (Retrieved: 24 December 2012).

Lenz, R. (2012). *Resurrection.* Intelligence Report. Winter 2012, Issue 148.

Levitas, D. (2002). *The Terrorist Next Door: The Militia Movement and the Radical Right.* Thomas Dunne Books.

Louis, B., Goldman, H., Christoff, C. (7 August 2012). *Wisconsin Sikh Shooting Suspect Formed Skinhead Bands.* Bloomberg. http://www.bloomberg.com/news/2012-08-06/wisconsin-sikh-shooting-probed-by-fbi-as-domestic-terror.html (Retrieved: 16 December 2012).

MacLean, N. (2010). "Neo-Confederacy versus the new deal: the regional Utopia of the modern American right." In Lassiter, M.W. and Crespino, J. (Eds.), *The Myth of Southern Exceptionalism.* Oxford University Press, New York, NY (Retrieved: 19 November 2009).

Martin, Gus (2011). *Terrorism and Homeland Security.* Sage Publications, Thousand Oaks, CA.

McFadden, C., Thompson, V., Meyersohn, J. (26 October 2012). *Klan Group Heralds Rise of New KKK, Calls for Segregation.* ABC Nightline. http://abcnews.go.com/US/klan-group-heralds-rise-kkk-calls-segregation/story?id = 17572788#.UMPEhI5y5UQ (Retrieved: 8 December 2012).

Memmott, M. (8 March 2012). *Report: "Explosive" Growth of "Patriot Movement" and Militias Continues.* NPR. http://www.npr.org/blogs/thetwo-way/2012/03/08/148217754/report-explosive-growth-of-patriot-movement-and-militias-continues (Retrieved: 29 December 2012).

Mohamed, F. (9 July 2011). *Kenya Enhances Airport Security.* Suna Times. http://sunatimes.com/view.php?id = 1160 (Retrieved: 28 December 2012).

Morgan, D. (2010). *Essential Islam: A Comprehensive Guide to Belief and Practice.* Praeger.

Morlin, B. (19 January 2012). *After Conviction, Kreis Quits as Leader of Tiny Aryan Nations Faction.* Southern Poverty Law Center. http://www.splcenter.org/blog/2012/01/19/after-conviction-kreis-quits-as-leader-of-tiny-aryan-nations-faction/ (Retrieved: 21 December 2012).

National Abortion Federation website. *Anti-Abortion Extremists: The Army of God and Justifiable Homicide.* http://www.prochoice.org/about_abortion/violence/army_god.html (Retrieved: 1 January 2013).

Nation of Islam website. *A Brief History on the origin of the Nation of Islam in America.* http://www.noi.org/about.shtml (Retrieved: 24 November 2012).

National Socialist Movement website. http://www.nsm88.org/aboutus.html (Retrieved: 15 December 2012).

Nazi Watch USA website (13 April 2007). *National Socialist Movement.* http://naziwatchusa.blogspot.com/2007/04/national-socialist-movement.htm (Retrieved: 15 December 2012).

"Neo-Nazism" (2002). Faculty of Humanities at Charles University in Prague, Department of Civil Society Studies. http://czechkid.eu/si1310.html (Retrieved: 2 December 2012).

Newton, M. and Ann, J. (Eds.), (1991). *The Ku Klux Klan: An Encyclopedia* (Vol. 499). Garland Publishing Inc., London/New York, NY.

North American Animal Liberation Front Press Office. *Frequently Asked Questions About the North American Animal Liberation Press Office.* http://animalliberationpressoffice.org/NAALPO/f-a-q-s/#8 (Retrieved: 2 January 2013).

Norton, M. and Sommers, S. (May 2011). *Whites see racism as a zero-sum game that they are now losing.* Perspectives on Psychological Science, 6(3), 215–218.

O'Connor, P., Allen, M. (6 November 2008). *Emanuel Accepts White House Job.* Politico. http://www.politico.com/news/stories/1108/15371.html (Retrieved: 8 December 2012).

Ottley, T. *Timothy McVeigh & Terry Nichols: Oklahoma Bombing.* Crime Library. http://www.trutv.com/library/crime/serial_killers/notorious/mcveigh/transit_6.html (Retrieved: 29 December 2012).

Pate, R. (2004). *The Anthrax Mystery: Solved.* National Vanguard, Issue 122.

Paul, R. (22 November 2012). *If People Cannot Secede, They Are Not Free.* Texas League of the South Website. http://texasls.org/2012/11/if-a-people-cannot-secede-they-are-not-free.html (Retrieved: 9 December 2012).

Philips, D. (22 August 1993). *Violence Hardly Ruffled Protest Ritual.* The Washington Post. http://www.washingtonpost.com/wp-srv/national/longterm/abortviolence/stories/tiller3.htm (Retrieved: 1 January 2013).

Phoenix Class War Council (15 October 2011). *The National Socialist Movement Scum Show Up Armed to Counter Protest #Occupyphoenix.* http://firesneverextinguished.blogspot.com/2011/10/national-socialist-movement-scum-show.html (Retrieved: 15 December 2012).

Pistole, J.S. (14 April 2004). *Statement Before the National Commission on Terrorist Attacks upon the United States.* http://govinfo.library.unt.edu/911/hearings/hearing10/pistole_statement.pdf (Retrieved: 24 May 2013).

Potok, M. (Spring 2012). *The Year in Hate & Extremism.* Southern Poverty Law Center, Intelligence Report, Issue 145.

Price, R. (2001). *Unholy War: America, Israel and Radical Islam.* Harvest House Publishers.

Pulaski, R. (23 March 2012). *New Black Panther Party Issues "Wanted Dead or Alive" Posters for George Zimmerman.* US Message Board. http://www.usmessageboard.com/race-relations-racism/214628-new-black-panther-party-issues-wanted-dead-or-alive-posters-for-george-zimmerman.html (Retrieved: 25 November 2012).

Qutb, S. (1998). *Milestones*. Bilal Books, Mumbai.

Reavis, D.J. (1995). *The Ashes of Waco: An Investigation*. Simon & Schuster, New York, NY.

Redmond, T. (29 May 2012). *FBI Is Scared of "Black Separatists."* San Francisco Bay Guardian Online. http://www.sfbg.com/politics/2012/05/29/fbi-scared-black-separatists (Retrieved: 2 December 2012).

Religious Tolerance website. *Christian Identity Movement*.http://www.religioustolerance.org/cr_ident. htm (Retrieved: 19 December 2012).

Research Staff of Vanguard Books (2004). *Who Rules America? The Alien Grip on Our News and Entertainment Media Must Be Broken*. The National Alliance website. http://www.natvan.com/ who-rules-america/index.html (Retrieved: 18 December 2012).

Ross, S. (10 October 2012). The CIA, the KKK and the USA. Veterans Today, Military & Foreign Affairs Journal. http://www.veteranstoday.com/2012/10/10/the-cia-the-kkk-and-the-usa/ (Retrieved: 9 December 2012).

Ryan, D. (10 December 2012). *Hate Crimes Down in 2011, but Anti-Gay Violence Up, FBI Says.* The Los Angeles Times. http://articles.latimes.com/2012/dec/10/nation/la-na-fbi-hate-crimes-20121211 (Retrieved: 31 December 2012).

Ryder, R.D. (2009). Speciesism. In Bekoff, M. (Ed.), *Encyclopedia of Animal Rights and Animal Welfare*.

Seale, B. (September 1997). Seize the Time *(Reprint ed.)*. Black Classic Press, pp. 23, 256, 383.

Senate Government Affairs Permanent Subcommittee on Investigations (31 October 1995). *Global Proliferation of Weapons of Mass Destruction: A Case Study on the Aum Shinrikyo*.https:// www.fas.org/irp/congress/1995_rpt/aum/part03.htm (Retrieved: 25 May 2013).

Schroeder, R. *Islam vs. the West: Why the Clash of Civilizations?* The Good News. http://www. ucg.org/news-and-prophecy/islam-vs-west-why-clash-civilizations/ (Retrieved: 23 December 2012).

Shahid, A. (7 April 2012). *Neo-Nazis Patrolling Streets of Sanford, Fla., Where Trayvon Shot and Killed*. New York Daily News. http://articles.nydailynews.com/2012-04-07/news/31306033_1_race-riots-racial-violence-usa-poll (Retrieved: 15 December 2012).

Schendel, S. *Since 2000, Lone-Offender Sovereign-Citizen Extremists Have Killed Six Law Enforcement Officers*. Murrow News Service. http://usnews.nbcnews.com/_news/2012/03/07/ 10602763-election-economy-spark-explosive-growth-of-militias?lite (Retrieved: 29 December 2012).

Schuster, H. (29 March 2005). *An Unholy Alliance. Aryan Nation Leader Reaches Out to al Qaeda*. CNN U.S. http://articles.cnn.com/2005-03-29/us/schuster.column_1_aryan-nation-qaeda-white-supremacists?_s = PM:US (Retrieved: 21 December 2012).

Shepherd, K. (14 October 2005). *Farrakhan's 9/11 Conspiracy Remarks Unreported by Washington Post*. Newsbusters: http://newsbusters.org/node/2210 (Retrieved: 24 November 2012).

Shell, E. (28 October 2011). *Ala.'s Sen. Beason on Aborigines, "the Clip."* PBS News Hour. http:// www.pbs.org/newshour/rundown/2011/10/alas-sen-beason-on-aborigines-the-clip.html (Retrieved: 31 December 2012).

Sinclair, M. (7 November 2007). *Profile of the New American Skinheads*. Inside NGC. http://incu-bator.nationalgeographic.com/inside_ngc/2007/11/profile-of-the-new-american-skinheads.html (Retrieved: 16 December 2012).

Sinuous Magazine (12 February 2011). *Reality Check, Latinos: You'll Never Be "White" Enough; Seeing Justice for Brisenia Flores*. http://www.sinuousmag.com/2011/02/seeking-justice-for-brise-nia-flores/ (Retrieved: 31 December 2012).

Skinheads Against Racial Prejudice: Champaign-Urbana Chapter website. http://www.cu-sharp. net/ (Retrieved: 16 December 2012).

Skinhead Nation (27 September 2007). *The Big Apple Bites Back.* Internet Archive Wayback Machine. http://web.archive.org/web/20070927212546/http://www.skinheadnation.co.uk/newyorks-kinheads.htm (Retrieved: 16 December 2012).

Smith, B. (5 July 2011). *Phoenix Man Gets 27 Years in Neighbor's Death.* Azcentral.com. http://www.azcentral.com/news/articles/2011/07/05/20110705phoenix-man-shoots-neighbor-sentence-abrk.html (Retrieved: 31 December 2012).

Smith, C.E. (2004). *Hate on Trial.* Southern Poverty Law Center. http://www.splcenter.org/get-informed/intelligence-report/browse-all-issues/2004/winter/hate-on-trial (Retrieved: 16 December 2012).

Snow, R.L. (2003). *Deadly Cults: The Crimes of True Believers.* Greenwood Publishing Group.

Southern Poverty Law Center (2011). *Inside the DHS: Former Top Analyst Says Agency Bowed to Political Pressure.* Intelligence Report, Summer 2011, Issue Number 42. http://www.splcenter.org/get-informed/intelligence-report/browse-all-issues/2011/summer/inside-the-dhs-former-top-analyst-says-agency-bowed (Retrieved: 22 November 2012).

Southern Poverty Law Center. *National Alliance.* http://www.splcenter.org/get-informed/intelligence-files/groups/national-alliance (Retrieved: 15 December 2012).

Southern Poverty Law Center. *New Black Panther Party.* http://www.splcenter.org/get-informed/intelligence-files/groups/new-black-panther-party (Retrieved: 25 November 2012).

Southern Poverty Law Center. *Hate Map.* http://www.splcenter.org/get-informed/hate-map (Retrieved: 25 November 2012).

Southern Poverty Law Center. *Jewish Defense League. http://www.splcenter.org/get-informed/intelligence-files/groups/jewish-defense-league#.UaFRY5Vy5UQ* (Retrieved: 25 May 2013).

Southern Poverty Law Center. *Keenan v. Aryan Nations.* http://www.splcenter.org/get-informed/case-docket/keenan-v-aryan-nations (Retrieved: 21 December 2012).

Southern Poverty Law Center. *Michael Hill.* Intelligence Files. http://www.splcenter.org/get-informed/intelligence-files/profiles/michael-hill (Retrieved: 9 December 2012).

Southern Poverty Law Center (2004). *Four Racist Skinheads Write Letters from Prison After Being Convicted of Brutal Killing.* http://www.splcenter.org/get-informed/intelligence-report/browse-all-issues/2004/summer/two-faces-of-volksfront/i-killed-him (Retrieved: 16 December 2012).

START—National Consortium for the Study of Terrorism and Responses to Terrorism. *Aryan Nations (AN). http://www.start.umd.edu/start/data_collections/tops/terrorist_organization_profile.asp?id = 29* (Retrieved: 21 December 2012).

Stormfront website (30 January 2002). *KKK Sees Surge in Recruitment Following 9/11, State Leader Says.* http://www.stormfront.org/forum/t11579/ (Retrieved: 9 December 2012).

Stormfront website. *14 Words.* http://www.stormfront.org/forum/t420259-3/ (Retrieved: 5 January 2013).

Stormfront website. *88 Precepts—David Lane.* http://www.stormfront.org/forum/t470316/ (Retrieved: 5 January 2013).

Streusand, D.E. (September 1997). *What does jihad mean?* The Middle East Quarterly, 4. (3). http://www.meforum.org/357/what-does-jihad-mean (Retrieved: 25 December 2012).

Stump, T.D. (19 October 2011). *Violent Anti-Immigrant Rhetoric: "It Will Kill You—Warning".* American Immigrant Lawyers Association, http://ailaleadershipblog.org/2011/10/19/violent-anti-immigrant-rhetoric-it-will-kill-you-warning/ (Retrieved: 31 December 2012).

Sullivan, E. (6 February 2012). *Sovereign Citizens Are Extremists Watched by FBI.* Huffington Post, http://www.huffingtonpost.com/2012/02/06/sovereign-citizens-are-threat_n_1258403.html (Retrieved: 26 December 2012).

Talk to Action website (19 September 2006). *FBI Ignores Antiabortion Terrorism...On 9/11.* http://www.talk2action.org/story/2006/9/19/3328/99097 (Retrieved: 1 January 2013).

Task Force on Confronting the Ideology of Radical Extremism (March 2009). *Rewriting the Narrative: An Integrated Strategy for Counterradicalization.* Washington Institute for Near East Policy, Washington, DC.

The Denver Post (18 June 2009). *The murder of Alan Berg in Denver: 25 Years Later.* http://www. denverpost.com/commented/ci_12615628 (Retrieved: 19 December 2012).

The Dr. Huey P. Newton Foundation. *There Is No New Black Panther Party: An Open Letter from the Dr. Huey P. Newton Foundation.* http://www.blackpanther.org/newsalert.htm (Retrieved: 24 November 2012).

The Insurgent (1 November 2012). *News and Views.* http://www.resist.com/updates/2012/NAV-20121101.html (Retrieved: 15 December 2012).

The Knights Party website (8 November 2012). *America's White Future Begins Here.* http://kkk. bz/ (Retrieved: 8 December 2012).

The National Alliance website. *National Alliance Goals.* http://www.natvan.com/what-is-na/na2. html#aryan (Retrieved: 18 December 2012).

U.S. Department of Homeland Security Assessment (7 April 2009). *Rightwing Extremism: Current Economic and Political Climate Fueling Resurgence in Radicalization and Recruitment.* http://www.fas.org/irp/eprint/rightwing.pdf.

U.S. Department of Justice, Federal Bureau of Investigation, Domestic Terrorism Operations Unit II (2010). *Sovereign Citizens: An Introduction for Law Enforcement.* http://publicintelligence. net/fbi-introduction-to-sovereign-citizens/

Walton, D. (1996). The straw man fallacy. In J. van Bentham, F.H. van Eemeren, R. Grootendorst and F. Veltman (Eds.), *Logic and Argumentation.* Royal Netherlands Academy of Arts and Sciences, North-Holland, Amsterdamhttp://www.dougwalton.ca/papers%20in%20pdf/96straw.pdf (Retrieved: 26 December 2012).

WebCite®. *Aryan Nations Website.* http://www.webcitation.org/5 × 8eOunHL (Retrieved: 21 December 2012).

Weiner, J., Curtis, H.P., Pavuk, A. (8 May 2012). *White Supremacists Trained with AK-47s, Planned for "Inevitable" Race War, Affidavit Says.* Orlando Sentinel. http://articles.orlandosenti-nel.com/2012-05-08/news/os-white-supremacist-arrests-osceola-20120507_1_crime-charges-conspiracy-charges-crime-and-criminal-conspiracy (Retrieved: 16 December 2012).

Wiktorowicz, Q. (2005). *Radical Islam Rising, Muslim Extremism in the West.* Rowman & Littlefield Publishers, Inc., Lanham, MD.

Williams, P. (28 January 2005). *Idaho Man Plotted to Kill 3 Federal Officials.* MSNBC News. http://www.rickross.com/reference/militia/militia89.html (Retrieved: 29 December 2012).

Wilogren, J. (9 January 2003). *White Supremacist Is Held in Ordering Judge's Death.* New York Times. http://blue.utb.edu/labad/white_supremacist_is_held_in_ord.htm (Retrieved: 21 December 2012).

Wordsmiths Compilation (2001). *The Jihad Fixation: Agenda, Strategy, Portents.* D.K. Print World Limited.

Yarbrough, T. (2008). *Harry A. Blackmun: The Outsider Justice.* Oxford University Press, New York, NY.

Zambelis, C. (11 August 2006). *Radical Trends in African-American Islam.* Terrorism Monitor, 4. (16). http://www.jamestown.org/programs/gta/single/?tx_ttnews%5Btt_news%5D = 872&tx_ttnews% 5BbackPid%5D = 181&no_cache = 1 (Retrieved: 28 December 2012).

Zelizer, J.E. (13 September 2010). *Bush Was Right: We're Not at War with Islam.* CNN Opinion. http://articles.cnn.com/2010-09-13/opinion/zelizer.bush.muslims_1_muslim-community-islamic-center-incredibly-valuable-contribution?_s = PM:OPINION (Retrieved: 24 December 2012).

CHAPTER 3

The Radicalization Pathway

With a clearer understanding of the kinds of ideological motivations that can attract and influence extremist views, it is possible to further investigate how an individual might shift from simply harboring extreme opinions and beliefs, to taking violent action in furtherance of their ideological aspirations or goals.

Most people who hold extremist views do not engage in violence. The proposition in this work is that the extremist ideology is embraced before, during and after activism. An examination of the radicalization process yields broader questions regarding how a person becomes engaged, stays engaged, or may actually disengage from the group and the ideology. Little attention has been given in the scholarly and policy literature to defining criteria for which extremist ideologies pose a threat to national or global security, or whether extremist ideologies matter at all in the absence of violent action. A 2009 U.S. Presidential Task Force on Confronting the Ideology of Radical Extremism recommends that the administration *expand* its focus from violent to nonviolent extremism.[1]

As noted in the Bipartisan Policy Center's *Preventing Violent Radicalization in America*, there is a difference between extremist ideas (*cognitive radicalization*) and extremist methods (*violent radicalization*).[2] Yet, the two are decisively connected. It is important to define the distinctions between extremist ideologies and methods so they can be examined in light of what is known, and guide what needs to be known, about the evolution from radicalization to violent extremism.[3]

Like the term "terrorism," radicalization is widely used but remains poorly defined. The term is often used as a synonym for extremist activities associated exclusively with Muslim Identity adherents.

---

[1]Task Force on Confronting the Ideology of Radical Extremism (March 2009). *Rewriting the Narrative: An Integrated Strategy for Counterradicalization.* Washington Institute for Near East Policy, Washington, DC.
[2]Lorenzo, V. (2010). *Countering Radicalization in America, Lessons from Europe.*
[3]Borum, R. (2011). *Radicalization into violent extremism I: a review of social science theories.* Journal of Strategic Security, 4(4), pp. 7–36.

This view, however, is shortsighted, in that it does not recognize that radicalization is a process that is not limited to any one ideology. Anyone can potentially traverse the radicalization pathway if the requisite mindset, ideology and environment are present.

In the context of this book, radicalization is the process through which individuals identify, embrace, and engage in furthering extremist ideologies and goals. It is important to note at the outset, however, that the radicalization pathway is not a fixed trajectory with specific, identifiable indicators that can be acknowledged on an itemized checklist of "suspicious activities." No single theory can comprehensively explain radicalization. Consequently, counterterrorism officials and policymakers must understand the overarching concept of radicalization and adopt interdisciplinary approaches when working to reduce opportunities for people to evolve from extremist adherent to violent actor.

The description of the radicalization pathway varies between countries, though there are some consistencies. Every nation and associated agency facing a threat from HVE is seeking commonality. Yet, despite the impetus to outline a terrorist profile or hallmarks of radicalization, empirical research has repeatedly concluded that there is no such profile and no easily identifiable representations. Government studies and scholars alike have highlighted the difficulty of predicting which individuals are likely to commit violent acts.

One of the most widely discussed radicalization pathway presentations on HVE in the post-9/11 era was the NYPD's 2007 report, *Radicalization in the West: The Homegrown Threat*. The study's objective was to understand "a point where we believe the potential terrorist or group of terrorists begin and progress through a process of radicalization. The culmination of this process is a terrorist attack."[4] In focusing on the human element in the equation, the effort sought to understand the process whereby "unremarkable" people become terrorists.[5]

The report assesses "Jihadist or jihadi-Salafi ideology" motivating young people, born or living in the West, to conduct terrorist attacks against their country of residence.[6] According to the NYPD assessment,

---

[4]Silber, M.D. and Arvin Bhatt (2007). *Radicalization in the West: The Homegrown Threat*. New York Police Department, Intelligence Division, p. 5.
[5]*Ibid*.
[6]*Ibid*. p. 6.

the radicalization process consists of four distinct phases: Pre-Radicalization, Self-Identification, Indoctrination and Jihadization.[7] The effort to understand this phenomenon was noble, but a number of other long-term studies have concluded that there are no such hallmarks of radicalization.

The NYPD report was championed and attacked in a variety of forums and on various levels, but it reveals a critical question about the radicalization process: Does radicalization depend on ideology? One way of answering this employs the theory of social movement mobilization. There is a popular notion, such as that used in the NYPD model, of an "ideas first" or a "center of gravity" continuum, whereby the extremist belief precedes the action. This is a concept in Ziad Munson's social movement theory, which offers three interpretations of the power of ideas.[8] Mobilization depends on:

- The degree to which a movement's ideology appeals to the existing beliefs (*framing theory*);
- Expressing a subculture's beliefs and identities (*new social movement theory*);
- Offering a substantial probability of social change in a favored direction (*rational choice theory*).

An alternative position, as proposed by Munson, suggests ideology is mostly learned in and after activism (e.g., attending a meeting or a worship service). One of the most interesting outcomes of the study (which looks specifically at pro-life activism) is that "activism does not mobilize only those with existing [beliefs]."[9] If activists are not mobilized only out of those with strong beliefs, how is an individual moved to activism?

Clark McCauley seeks to explain this progression in four-step process (where no step is a prerequisite for the next).[10]

1. There is a contact with a stream of the movement that comes at a "turning point," when the individual's everyday life is changing because of a significant personal adjustment.

---

[7] *Ibid.*
[8] Munson, Z. (2008). *The Making of Pro-Life Activists: How Social Movement Mobilization Works.*
[9] *Ibid.*
[10] McCauley, C. (2009). *Does political radicalization depend on ideology?* Dynamics of Asymmetric Conflict, 2(3), 213–215.

2. The individual participates in some kind of activism, such as a meeting, a protest, a counseling session or a rally.
3. There is a development of considered and consistent beliefs. This is entirely consistent with social psychological experiments demonstrating the human tendency to find reasons for what we do.[11]
4. The individual engages in regular and routinized participation in a stream of activism.

One of the most interesting observations noted by McCauley is the consideration of religion in this transformative pathway. He notes that "participation in a [group] can provide contact with activists—only rarely does activism emerge directly from a conversion experience. More often, activists acquire deeper religious beliefs in the course of activist experience. Munson's comparisons of activists and nonactivists found no difference in religiosity or religious activities."[12]

While preexisting beliefs are not a prerequisite for activism, there are certainly factors that can make an individual more susceptible to radicalization, or at least, facilitate the process. An analysis by the National Counterterrorism Center (NCTC) suggests these factors arise on five distinct levels.[13] These are *personal-level* (psychological issues, demographic backgrounds, personal history); *group-level* (social networks, group dynamics); *community-level* (alienation, marginalization, diaspora relationships); *sociopolitical-level* (collective grievances, foreign policy and external events); and *ideological-level* (appeal of a justifying narrative, charismatic ideologues).[14]

It is a combination of factors that ultimately contribute to a person's vulnerability to the radicalization process. Independently, any one of these factors will not necessarily lead an individual to violence, but when joined, they could produce a higher likelihood. Yet, given that the number of nonviolent extremists vastly outnumbers those who are violent, even a combination of factors cannot fully explain why some individuals turn violent while others do not.

---

[11]Aronson, E. (1969). *The theory of cognitive dissonance: a current perspective.* In L. Berkowitz (Ed.), *Advances in Experimental Social Psychology.*
[12]McCauley, C. (2009). *Does political radicalization depend on ideology?* Dynamics of Asymmetric Conflict, 2(3), 213–215.
[13]National Counterterrorism Center (June 2012). *Radicalization Dynamics, A Primer.*
[14]*Ibid.*

3.1 COMPONENTS OF THE RADICALIZATION PROCESS

All attempts to model the human element and identify one's propensity toward radicalization or mobilization-to-violence have invariably failed. Nevertheless, radicalization factors point to a number of complex, supportive issues that facilitate the development of a terrorist. In concurrence with Louise Richard's work in the area, the road to violent extremism is cleared by three essential components: an alienated and altruistic individual; a legitimizing ideology; and an enabling community.[15]

3.1.1 Alienated and Altruistic Individuals

A central component in the process is a sense of alienation from the existing state of affairs, accompanied by a sense of altruism, as well as a desire and belief that the *status quo* can be changed. How does the feeling develop and when is an individual most susceptible to a new narrative that fills the void and provides hope for fulfilling a new purpose?

Extremist thought and action operate on individual, group and organizational levels. Individuals contribute *inspiration and commitment* to the advancement of the political objective; groups facilitate the community component, enabling *socialization into the extremist ideologies*; and organizations provide the *structure and internal processes* essential for group sustainability.

Terrorist and extremist organizations present ideologies as noble causes, promising to fulfill their supporters' social and psychological needs. Although the difference between "terrorist" and "extremist" groups may be their respective active or passive support of violence (e.g., Irish Republican Army versus Sinn Féin), terrorist groups characteristically express active engagement, while extremist organizations offer disclaimers articulating the lack of endorsement of violent acts. Yet, the desired outcomes of both kinds of groups (to attract adherents willing to embrace the ideology in furtherance of the political objectives) are indistinguishable.

Potential adherents are often socially alienated individuals, estranged from their communities, who have chosen to distance

[15]Richardson, L. (2006). *What Terrorists Want, Understanding the Enemy, Containing the Threat.* Random House. New York, NY.

themselves from others, even those who may be important to them, such as family members and friends. This alienation from mainstream society, culture or government policies prepares an individual for an interest in extremist ideology.

An examination of a number of violent extremists in the post-9/11 era indicates that "distancing" is a common factor. For example, al Qaeda spokesperson Adam Gadahn, al Qaeda's *Inspire* Editor-in-Chief Samir Kahn, and Boston bomber Tamerlan Tsarnaev all separated from their mosques and families before departing the United States or committing a terrorist act. Given that there are alienated individuals in any group or community, however, what further propels an individual to engage in violence?

One explanation may be personalities on the edge of the group (*the fringe*) who have adopted the ideology in a manner that requires a demonstration of their commitment through violence. Extremist groups find these individuals most attractive. In the militia movement, "those most inclined toward violence sometimes call themselves Three Percenters, a small vanguard that dares to match deeds to words."[16] This notion of Three Percenters comes from Mike Vanderboegh, based on the concept that about 3% of the population fought for independence during the Revolutionary War.[17] The violence-prone fringe element is seeking an ideological common ground when joining an extremist group whose foundational beliefs are not identical to their own.

3.1.2 Legitimizing Ideology

The perception of a grievance, such as conflicted identities, injustice, oppression or socioeconomic exclusion, can make people receptive to extremist ideas.[18] These moments often arise during a crisis, be it a personal experience or one with which the subject identifies. This can inspire an individual to adopt an extremist narrative or ideology that addresses their grievance and offers a rationale for action.[19] A crisis can produce what Quintan Wiktorowicz calls a "cognitive opening."

[16]Gellman, B. (30 September 2010). *The Secret World of Extreme Militias*. Time Magazine.
[17]Three Percenter website. About Three Percenter.
[18]Wiktorowicz, Q. (2005). *Radical Islam Rising, Muslim Extremism in the West*.
[19]Brachman, J. (2005). *Global Jihadism: Theory and Practice*. Routledge, London and New York, pp. 52−78.

Previously-held beliefs are shaken, making an individual receptive to alternative ideas.[20]

The crisis that prompts a cognitive opening is not exclusive to any one of the HVE motivations (race, religion or issue orientation), but there are some common types, like economic, social or cultural challenges, and political repression or discrimination.[21] Personal situations also yield cognitive openings, produced by idiosyncratic experiences, such as a death in the family or victimization by crime. This is particularly critical if the personal situation is perceived to have been caused by the U.S. government.

The rationale for embracing an ideology, much like the radicalization process itself, is complex and perhaps unique to the adherent. Embracing the ideology, however, is as complicated as understanding the psychology of group dynamics. The necessary sustainability to fuel an act of terrorism requires reinforcement from the group. Stern notes that some individuals join extremist groups out of ideological conviction and later become violent as the emotional or material benefits become more important than the beliefs.[22]

3.1.3 Enabling Community

Cognitive openings may be leveraged when economic, social, cultural, political, and personal situations are recognized as traumatic and may be exploited. In these situations, a supportive environment (group or community) can facilitate overt or passive recruitment of the affected individuals by using the influence of the group members or their leadership. In an examination of this dynamic, scholar Jerrold Post interviewed 35 imprisoned Middle Eastern terrorists and found a process that yields an overarching sense of the collective and consensus on contributory characteristics for cognitive openings. In South Asia, there is another example, where religion and promises of paradise in the afterlife have nothing to do with those who volunteer to be suicide terrorists. Sri Lanka is the home of the Liberation Tigers of Tamil Eelam (LTTE) or Tamil Tigers, the separatist militant organization that made suicide terrorism an integral component of their strategy. LTTE adherents join to pursue revenge, to take part in national liberation

---

[20]Wiktorowicz, *Radical Islam Rising.*
[21]*Ibid.*
[22]Stern, J. (2010). *Mind over Martyr: how to deradicalize Islamist extremists.* Foreign Affairs, 89 (1), 103.

and even for self-glorification. They have been "personally affected by the conflict in which they live, because their community supports their action, and because their movement's ideology legitimizes it."[23]

The nature of the political objectives and the relationship to the broader community are critically important to the psychology of the enabling environment. Post concludes there are demonstrable psychological differences between those who are furthering the work of their parents (*ethnonationalist groups*) and those who are trying to destroy the world of their parents (*social revolutionary groups*).[24] The lifespan of these two groups are somewhat predictable.

Ethnonationalist terrorist groups are able to endure because of their close ties to the supportive community. Thus, the ideology and associated behaviors develop over time and are not always considered extreme. Conversely, social revolutionary groups tend not to have an "external source of information or security, nor any perspective with which to question the dictates of the movement."[25] As a result, the isolated nature of these groups facilitates the creation of their own desired sense of reality, requiring limited external input that would put into question the rationality of their ideology.

For both social revolutionaries and ethnonationalists, supportive and complicit environments are important infrastructure for broad-based, ideological movements. In many cases, the broader community shares a terrorist group's goals, though they may not endorse the methods for meeting them.[26] The development of "compounds" in several locations and associated with a variety of groups across the country serve as extreme illustrations of complicit communities. In other cases, the greater community is aware of particular extremist activities and knowingly allows them to grow. This passive support is essentially an endorsement, inasmuch as restraints are nonexistent.

The twenty-first century provided a new foundation for the enabling community—online, open source extremism. The use of the Internet is

[23]Richardson, Louise (2006). *What Terrorists Want, Understanding the Enemy, Containing the Threat.*

[24]Post, Jerrold M. (1984). *Notes on a Psychodynamic Theory of Terrorist Behavior.* Terrorism: An International Journal 7, 3: 242–256.

[25]Richardson, L. (2006). *What Terrorists Want, Understanding the Enemy, Containing the Threat,* p. 49

[26]*Ibid.*

perhaps the most dangerous extremist and terrorist radicalization and recruitment innovation since 9/11. Online radicalization facilitates the sharing of ideas and tactics, it develops and enhances social networks, it conscripts new recruits, and it may inspire illegal and violent action. *Inspire* magazine (which exists exclusively online) targets U.S. and other Western governments by motivating homegrown terrorists. The dissemination of their so-called auto-propaganda was intended to encourage community support for al Qaeda's ideology.

Given the central role of a complicit community in the radicalization process, it is important to examine the morality, leadership and group behavioral constructs capable of supporting a terrorism-resistant community model.

3.2 THE ROLE OF MORAL PRINCIPLE

Louise Richardson describes an enabling ("complicit") society that facilitates terrorist operational activities (e.g., employment, travel, and most importantly, living within a community perhaps at greater risk of extremist recruitment). To most accurately understand the notion of complicity, the issues with which communities must grapple are those of morality and cultivating a moral society.

Morality is characterized as "proper behavior" and used normatively, "morality refers to a code of conduct that applies to all who can understand it and can govern their behavior by it."[27] Diverse societies have come to interpret these codes differently, particularly as they relate to issues of law, religious practices and community etiquette. Yet, morality is not a guide for everyone to follow. It is a code that may be offered by an individual for consideration by the larger community.

Noam Chomsky writes that one of the most common moral principles is universality: "If something's right for me, it's right for you; if it's wrong for you, it's wrong for me."[28]

[27]Gert, B., *The Definition of Morality. The Stanford Encyclopedia of Philosophy (Summer 2011 Edition)*, Edward N. Zalta (Ed.). Retrieved: http://plato.stanford.edu/archives/sum2011/entries/morality-definition/.
[28]Chomsky, N. (2007). Responsibility and War Guilt, Conference Interview with Noam Chomsky, The Massachusetts Institute of Technology.

The discussion of morality in the normative context presents an opportunity for a community developed code of conduct. Morality in the normative sense describes an accepted code of conduct that the group agrees to abide by and offers no ambiguity. For example, theft in society in general and in the FBI Academy specifically is understood to be morally wrong. The fact that dormitory doors at the Academy would not have locks implies an Academy morality in the normative sense that locks are unnecessary because theft would not occur. This is reinforced by the fact that rationality in these instances is assumed. As a result, all rational people would endorse a code of conduct, as in the case of the FBI Academy dormitory having no concern for theft as a moral code.

The importance of communities, like the residents of the FBI Academy or other similar environments, is the understanding that neighborhoods have the capacity to establish their own respective morality. In that sense, there could be a code of conduct developed and implemented by the affected community regarding behaviors deemed unacceptable. Unlike the public safety laws already in place, these codes would address additional concerns determined by the "community" in an effort to eliminate or at least reduce the risk of occurrence. Public safety is understandably reasonably easy to endorse, but extremist behaviors including hate speech, intolerance and other extremist characteristics would be more challenging, unless determined to be part of the community morality. Communities embracing morality normatively would simultaneously articulate their intolerance for extremist behaviors that violate the code.

3.3 THE ROLE OF LEADERSHIP IN RADICALIZATION

Social science research examines the underlying laws of human behavior and is geared toward evidence-based information. These analyses focus on the notion of testable hypothesis about human behavior. While there are many factors that contribute to societal morality, with regard to radicalization, leadership has a significant impact.

Leadership associated with the disparate extremist ideologies can be but are not necessarily critical to messaging success. There are instances when a group leader connects with the person seeking meaning and provides an opportunity and environment in which they can learn about an extremist ideology. A U.K. Home Office study evaluating what makes an individual more vulnerable to al Qaeda-influenced violent extremism, concludes that charismatic individuals play an important role, delivering the persuasive ideology while also helping individuals join an extremist group.[29]

These charismatic leaders offer a unique opportunity for potential recruits to prove themselves to someone they admire. This may be particularly true for individuals who have previously failed to establish a positive identity and status in school, work, sports, or other social activities and settings. Association with a group and embracing an extremist ideology legitimizes their efforts to earn respect and contribute to a cause. Extremist characteristics like intolerance, superiority, "otherism," moral absolutes, generalizations lacking foundation, doomsday scenarios, conspiracy theories, and code speak are at the core of leadership outreach, in part because they can offer an attractive context through which an individual understands their crisis, helping to mitigate or make sense of a cognitive dilemma or personal trauma.

Conversely, the U.K. study also showed research that highlights the potential for terrorist groups to develop *without* a clear leader or central figure. Marc Sageman found no evidence of a formal top-down recruitment of individuals to terrorist groups, with like-minded individuals forming groups that go on to become more extreme in their views.[30] Looking for the common bond for group cohesion, he conducted a social network analysis of 400 terrorists connected with the 1998 embassy bombings in Kenya and Tanzania, who targeted the United States as opposed to their own governments.

Sageman found the majority were college-educated (63%), from upper- or middle-class families (75%), and whose families were caring and intact (90%). Family and job responsibilities were also apparent, as 73% were married and most had children. They were not religious initially. Rather, 70% *became* religious after leaving their home country. Becoming homesick, they drifted toward the local mosque, seeking friendship more than religion. Exposure to more militant scripts advocating violence to overthrow corrupt regimes transformed their relationships and their goals. Group dynamics developed in this way tend

[29]UK Home Office (2011). *Understanding Vulnerability and Resilience in Individuals to the Influence of Al Qa'ida Violent Extremism, A Rapid Evidence Assessment to Inform Policy and Practice in Preventing Violent Extremism.* Office for Security and Counter-Terrorism.
[30]Sageman, M. (2004). *Understanding Terror Networks.*

to operate independently, rather than receiving orders from a central command.

While a central leader is not a prerequisite for radicalization, a charismatic leader can play a fundamental role in the process. There are a number of leadership styles, and the type that leaders adopt is based on their core beliefs, values, and preferences. The resulting leadership action is designed to influence the community norms and culture. There is no comprehensive style that addresses all circumstances present in a community. Given the dynamic and complex nature of recruitment, radicalization and retention of violent extremists, a hybridized version of the three leadership styles discussed below (transformational, situational and charismatic) equips a leader with the tools to appeal to a broad audience.

3.3.1 Transformational Leadership

Transformational leadership is based on the premise that change is essential and the *status quo* must be eliminated. Transformational individuals are people of action, embracing an understanding for urgency in the need for progress. Yet, transformational leadership does not necessarily lead to positive change. Suicide bombers, for example, believe they are acting in ways that facilitate the greater good. Historically, there have been a number of transformational leaders who believed in their own brand of progress, accomplished to the detriment of others. Individuals like Adolf Hitler, Genghis Khan, Mao Tse-Tung, and Joseph Stalin are a few whose transformational objectives were achieved by indoctrinating or killing the opposition. Thus, it seems transformational leaders operate at great personal risk of resistance and defeat from without and within.

Researcher Bernard Bass expanded on these ideas in his Transformational Leadership Theory.[31] For Bass, transformational leadership holds four primary elements: "individualized consideration, intellectual stimulation, inspirational motivation and idealized influence."[32] He also identifies charisma and vision as defining qualities. It is interesting that the most defining and recurring quality mentioned in a diverse collection of leadership styles is also the most difficult to define—charisma.

---

[31]Bass, B. (1985). *Leadership and Performance*. Free Press, New York, NY.
[32]Bass, B. and Bruce Avolio (1994). *Improving Organizational Effectiveness Through Transformational Leadership*. SAGE Publications.

3.3.2 Situational Leadership

The Hershey–Blanchard Situational Leadership Theory (created by Paul Hershey and Ken Blanchard) suggests that successful leaders change leadership styles to suit their audience's maturity and the specifics of the task.[33] The theory is based on *Task Behavior* and *Relationship Behavior*, provided to the group by the leader. Leadership can be categorized into four behavior types:[34]

1. *Telling* – Characterized by one-way communication in which the leader defines the roles of the individual or group and provides the what, how, why, when, and where to do the task.
2. *Selling*—The leader uses two-way communication and provides the socio-emotional support that allows the individual or group to buy in to the process.
3. *Participating*—The leader engages in a participative style to accomplish the task, less delegation of tasks to the group while maintaining a high relationship with them.
4. *Delegating*—The leader is involved in decisions and monitors progress, but the process and responsibility is passed to the individual or group.

The Hersey–Blanchard Situational Leadership Theory is most effective when leaders understand the audience's maturity level. There are four primary maturity levels: [35]

1. *M1*—Individuals lack the knowledge, skills, or confidence to work on their own, and they often need to be pushed to take on a task.
2. *M2*—Followers might be willing to work on the task but lack the skills to do it successfully.
3. *M3*—Followers are ready and willing to help with the task, possessing more skills than the M2 group but lacking confidence in their abilities.
4. *M4*—Followers are able to work on their own, have high confidence and strong skills, and are committed to the task.

---

[33]Hersey, P. (1984). *The Situational Leader.* Center for Leadership Studies, Binghamton University, New York, NY.
[34]Mind Tools™. *The Hersey–Blanchard Situational Leadership®Theory Choosing the Right Leadership Style for the Right People.* Retrieved: http://www.mindtools.com/pages/article/newLDR_44.htm.
[35]*Ibid.*

The subsequent model maps the aforementioned leadership styles with appropriate maturity levels that best yield the desired outcome:

Leadership Engagement	Maturity Level
S1: Telling/Directing	M1: Low maturity
S2: Selling/Coaching	M2: Medium maturity, limited skills
S3: Participating/Supporting	M3: Medium maturity, higher skills but lacking confidence
S4: Delegating	M4: High maturity

Ali al-Timimi, a former biologist and Islamic scholar born in Washington, DC, demonstrated tremendous range in leadership engagement in the way he recruited followers to join the Taliban to fight U.S. troops. Timimi, who had an international following, was described as enjoying "rock star status"[36] among a group of followers in Virginia. Despite his academic acumen and global reach, he understood the importance of building trust from the ground up. Inasmuch as his followers could be described as possessing "medium maturity," and lacked the confidence or background to consider joining a war effort overseas, Timimi embarked on a "participating/supporting" engagement. He facilitated their recruitment by holding regular paintball outings. Although the followers were told they were preparing for holy war around the globe, Timimi realized the potential of the relationship building outcomes. Although none of the followers ultimately joined the Taliban, four of the men traveled to Pakistan just weeks after the 9/11 attacks and trained with the Kashmir-focused Lashkar-e-Taiba (LT). Timimi was subsequently convicted of inciting terrorism and sentenced to life imprisonment.

3.3.3 Charismatic Leadership

Charisma is a constant for leaders responsible for significant change. It is an essential character trait supporting other leadership styles, sometimes employed as a style in its own right. Skillful and influential charismatic leaders appeal to their audience's values, which is what allows them to succeed.[37] German political economist, legal historian and sociologist Max Weber viewed charisma as consistent with the concept of genius. Referring to charisma as a "gift of grace," he

[36]Barakat, M. (27 April 2005). *Islamic Scholar Convicted of Advocating War on US.* The Boston Globe.
[37]Palshikar, K. *Charismatic Leadership.* Retrieved: www.unc.edu/~ketan/documents/Charismatic%20Leadership.pdf.

described charismatic leaders as self-appointed individuals "who are followed by those who are in distress and who need to follow the leader because they believe him to be extraordinarily qualified."[38] This leadership mode fosters follower empowerment of the kind required to embrace harsh tactics necessary for significant social change. It is this kind of political outcome that validates and legitimizes the ideology and the subsequent violent action.

Charismatic leadership is often a component of a diverse collection of leadership styles. The danger associated with this style is the development of a group emboldened by a superiority mindset. In a number of racial, religious and issue-oriented extremist ideologies, this is in fact the intended outcome. Given a range of ideologies, organizational objectives and the political context in which an extremist group is developed, adherents' attraction rests on their embrace of the message and the messenger. As the group develops and matures, the charismatic leader aligns their identity with that of the group. In that regard, group membership and allegiance to the leader essentially become one and the same. While extremist thought operates on individual, group and organizational levels, the element that binds is leadership.

Interest is garnered and sustained inasmuch as the leader is viewed as interpreting the ideology, deciphering the complexity of related issues and offering feasible remedies, often with violent responses to the identified challenges. Individual needs are met as the ideology gains clarity, the process of socialization enhances group dynamics and the organization provides the critical element of structure to one's life. A hybrid of leadership styles is most effective in accomplishing this progression, if an individual who is savvy enough to implement the appropriate style delivers it at the ideal time.

Anwar al-Awlaki is an example of extraordinary leadership appeal. Although his American heritage removed the potential for actual organizational leadership with core al Qaeda, his charismatic attraction came as a result of demonstrating scholarship, patience and consistent messaging. His ability to hybridize his leadership style was demonstrated in his personal and virtual encounters, as he provided spiritual guidance to several 9/11 hijackers and by working online, enlisted a cadre of followers around the world (whom he never met).

---

[38]Weber, M. (1991). *From Max Weber: Essays in Sociology*. Psychology Press, p. 52.

Al-Awlaki's demonstration of hybrid leadership illustrates the remarkable outcome potential when the appropriate leadership engagement is matched with the corresponding maturity level. The ability to move between leadership engagements requiring directing, coaching, supporting, and delegating to an audience of low, medium, and high maturity levels demonstrates his capacity and the importance of truly understanding leadership on a cognitive level.

3.4 THE ROLE OF GROUP BEHAVIOR

History and research have demonstrated that groups, motivated by their ideology, moral code, convenience or survival, can be negatively influenced to violent ends. Hostile actions against those not within a group is not only accepted but morally and legally sanctioned. Such is the case in Myanmar, where the homegrown neo-Nazi Buddhist movement, 969, led by fascist, skinhead monks is engaged in an ethnic cleansing of Rohingya Muslims. The fact that Muslim pilgrims have been slaughtered in broad daylight, with no arrests, speaks to the apparent complicity of the Myanmar government security forces, the media and the majority community, who are supportive of a pure Buddhist state.

A community's capacity to reduce the risk of radicalization requires group behaviors and appropriate leadership coalescing to establish community consensus on the immorality of violent extremist behaviors. Consensus on this issue of community action, as it relates to the social network engaged in the life of the HVE actor, cannot be overstated. Recalling that terrorism requires an alienated individual following a legitimizing ideology, operating within an enabling, complicit society, it is the community that is most susceptible to positive influence proposed by a risk-reduction model.

There are a number of theories on group decision making. Group problem analysis and proper leadership can be managed to induce positive outcomes but only if appropriate consensus building processes are in place to facilitate the identification and selection of intelligent alternatives to violent extremism. The essence of counterterrorism policies is based on reducing the risk and containing the threat of an attack. Community engagement is critical to reducing that risk. A comparative analysis of relevant theoretical structures helps reveal their capacity to engender positive moral group actions and counter malicious activity.

3.4.1 Groupthink

Particularly as it relates to the risk of HVE, decision process characteristics are the underpinnings of meaningful efforts toward community safety. Yale University research psychologist Irving Janis focused on the concept of *groupthink*. Janis defined the term as "a mode of thinking that people engage in when they are deeply involved in a cohesive ingoup, when the members' striving for unanimity override their motivation to realistically appraise alternative courses of action."[39] He documented eight symptoms of groupthink:

1. *Illusion of invulnerability*—Creates excessive optimism that encourages extreme risk taking.
2. *Collective rationalization*—Members discount warnings and do not reconsider their assumptions.
3. *Belief in inherent morality*—Members believe in the rightness of their cause and ignore the ethical or moral consequences of their decisions.
4. *Stereotyped views of out-groups*—Negative views of the "enemy" eliminate the need or desire to respond to dissenting opinions.
5. *Direct pressure on dissenters*—Members are under pressure not to express arguments against any of the group's views.
6. *Self-censorship*—Doubts and deviations from the perceived group consensus are not expressed.
7. *Illusion of unanimity*—The majority view and judgments are assumed to be unanimous.
8. *Self-appointed "mindguards"*—Members protect the group and the leader from information that is problematic or contradictory to the group's cohesiveness, view and/or decisions.[40]

The forfeiture of a person's individual thoughts or original concepts is a desired outcome of HVE leadership, as they strive to exploit potential cognitive openings detected in those subjects seeking additional knowledge regarding the respective ideology. The resultant community environment is one of collective optimism accompanied by collective avoidance, as the group molds its thinking to reflect the majority consensus.

[39]Janis, I. (1972). *Victims of Groupthink: a Psychological Study of Foreign-Policy Decisions and Fiascoes*. Houghton Mifflin, Boston, MA.
[40]Hart, P. (1998). *Preventing groupthink revisited: evaluating and reforming groups in government*. Organizational Behavior and Human Decision Processes, 73: 306–326.

There have been several social science experiments that tested the power of community impact on decision making. Social scientist Solomon Asch designed an experiment to determine the extent to which group pressure could be exerted to influence an individual's perception. In the experiment, participants were given two cards. One card held a single vertical line; the second held several. Participants were asked which vertical line in the second card matched the length of the vertical line in the first.

Participants were told the experiment was being conducted to test visual acuity and each of the students was asked to provide their answers aloud. All but one of the students, labeled "confederates," were instructed to give correct and incorrect answers in the initial trials and to provide exclusively incorrect responses in "staged" trials. Asch designed the seating arrangement so that the real subject was the next-to-the-last person to respond in each group.

The results showed that one-third of responses followed the erroneous majority, while there were almost no errors in the control group: "some subjects always defied the group, some always went along with them. Twenty-five percent were completely independent, 33% were more than half with the erroneous majority."[41]

Asch surmised that the tendency to conform outweighs intelligence and perception.[42] Continued research identified and quantified the situational factors that influence conformity, such as group size and cohesiveness. For Asch, individuals conform for two primary reasons: because they want to be liked by the group; and because they believe the group is better informed.[43]

As another example of how community thinking influences individual behavior, Yale University psychologist Stanley Milgram's now-famous experiment was designed to measure the compliance of study participants to obey instructions from an authority figure to inflict

---

[41] Asch, S.E. (1951). *Effects of Group Pressure Upon the Modification and Distortion of Judgments.* In H. Guetzkow (Ed.) Groups, Leadership, and Men. Retrieved: http://faculty.babson.edu/krollag/org_site/soc_psych/asch_conform.html.
[42] Solomon Asch experiment (1958). A study of conformity. Retrieved: http://www.age-of-the-sage.org/psychology/social/asch_conformity.html.
[43] *Ibid.*

pain (electric shocks) on others, even when those individuals begged not to be shocked.[44]

The *theory of conformism*, based on Asch's work, was a key factor in explaining the group decisions observed in Milgram's experiment. The theory of conformism explains how the participants, lacking decision-making authority, will leave the decision to the group and its hierarchy. Thus, the group becomes the participant's behavioral model.

Milgram concluded that any individual can become an agent in a "terrible destructive process. Moreover, even when the destructive effects of their work become patently clear, and they are asked to carry out actions incompatible with fundamental standards of morality, relatively few people have the resources needed to resist authority."[45] Thus, it becomes increasingly clear how HVE adherents, despite an acceptance of morality in the normative sense, will respond without question to directions from strong leadership. The task of furthering the ideological political objective at all costs, accompanied by the acknowledgment of the associated catastrophic human losses, illustrates the conflict between basic human morals and the HVE mission.

3.4.2 Groupthink and HVE

The racist, right-wing cult, the Covenant, Sword and the Arm of the Lord (CSA), demonstrates the power of groupthink socialization and the potentially deadly outcomes. Kerry Noble, CSA's second in command, has revealed much about the CSA radicalization process and the group's goal of overthrowing the U.S. government. Now separated from the violent Christian Identity movement, Noble's book (*Tabernacle of Hate, Why They Bombed Oklahoma City*) and lectures provide unique insight into why people join and may come to disengage from violent extremist groups.

Predicated on a doomsday scenario, the CSA engaged its followers in several critical steps to develop unquestionable loyalty to their beliefs. Generally, people who ultimately join extremist movements are

[44]Milgram, S. (1974). *Obedience to Authority: An Experimental View.* HarperCollins Publishers, New York, NY.
[45]Milgram, S. (1974). *The Perils of Obedience.* Harper's Magazine. Abridged and adapted from *Obedience to Authority.*

searching for something. In the case of CSA, its deeply religious foundation seduced followers into accepting the scripted responses to their important questions on faith. CSA's charismatic leadership, invoked by Jim Ellison, explained that everything a person would want to know is based in scripture. Ellison's faith was based on the knowledge that God was directing him and the group.

Ellison's patience with group members was extraordinary, inviting questions but always delivering definitive and final responses to their queries. He explained that innocuous things seen or heard during the course of their daily routing—numbers, letters and seemingly unimportant phrases—all had a nexus to scripture, and those who understood and followed his guidance would someday see their loyalty rewarded.

A critical first step in the CSA radicalization process involved a sense of "oneness" with God. Members were told individuality was counterproductive. Only when the members divested personal artifacts and separated from the past, becoming one "Body," could they hope to allow God to accomplish his mission through them. Acknowledging the "Body" was most important—group members sold everything of value. They burned photos. Men shaved their heads and swore allegiance to CSA. Cultivating this sense of oneness is a common practice among extremist groups and cults, as it consequently facilitates groupthink.

One of CSA's final radicalization steps included societal isolation. CSA is emblematic of other isolationist extremist groups, choosing to build compounds, home school their children with a curriculum that implanted the ideology, and eventually, identify an enemy. In this case, the enemy was the government, causing CSA to initiate weapons and tactics training under the guise of preparing to defend themselves on the prophesized day of destruction. The societal isolation was enhanced by allowing only limited and filtered information to reach the group. This was accomplished by removing all sources of media from the environment. Thus, the stage was set. The CSA had its savior, an ideology and an enemy.

The CSA groupthink mentality was based on hate, a common ideology for HVE groups. Circling the wagons against their adversaries, the battle lines were drawn—Jews were controlling the country's financial systems; Blacks, supported by welfare, were destroying America's cities; and

Asians were taking the remaining high-paying jobs. CSA legitimized its ideology with the support of the U.S. Constitution, declaring income tax was illegal, allowing them to avoid paying taxes, and the Second Amendment provided legal justification to possess unregistered machine guns. These beliefs and practices facilitated hate based on cultivation of fear from perceived threats, a hallmark characteristic of HVE groups.

Ultimately, CSA's foundational premise of becoming the "Body" was extolled using common extremist group characteristics, including intolerance, moral absolutes, generalizations lacking foundation, doomsday scenarios and code speak. The standoff between CSA and government agencies on April 19, 1985, would have been a bloody disaster were it not for Noble, who by this time was at odds with Ellison. Noble challenged CSA's hypocrisy; its criminal (including terrorist) activities, which included murder, bombings and robberies; and the obsession with setting doomsday dates for the destruction of the nation, such as August 1978, spring 1979 and summer 1979. Despite the psychological pressure bearing on the group, they coalesced around Ellison's leadership and were ready to die when the time came. Noble concluded that it was the controlled inflow of information and the isolation from society that facilitated CSA's notion of group safety, security and sanity. Were it not for his uncommon rejection of a group of which he was a part and desire for peaceful negotiation, the 1985 standoff could have ended much differently and with a great deal of bloodshed.

3.4.3 General Group Problem Solving Model

The General Group Problem Solving (GGPS)-Model is a four-phase process developed in response to the limited focus and isolated framing of existing group decision-making models. The phases consist of Antecedents, Emergent Group Characteristics, Decision Process Characteristics and Outcomes.[46]

The lack of real-world application (versus theoretical frameworks) was an important issue in a broader context as proposed by GGPS authors Aldag and Fuller. They claim that "the groupthink model is overly deterministic and an unrealistically restrictive depiction of the

---

[46]Aldag, R.J. and Fuller, S.R. (2001). The GGPS model: broadening the perspective on group problem solving. In M. Turner (Ed.), *Groups at Work: Theory and Research*. Lawrence Erlbaum Ass, Mahwah, NJ.

group problem-solving process."[47] In other words, the methodology of the GGPS-Model is designed to identify the desired outcome, identify the gap(s) between the goal and the current situation, and design a plan to achieve the objective.

The advantages and shortcomings of groupthink, such as cohesiveness, homogeneity, insulation and leader impartiality, are identified characteristics in the "Group Structure" component of the GGPS-Model's "Antecedent" phase. However, the potential advantages of the GGPS-Model are revealed in the subsequent phase—Emergent Group Characteristics.

The model identifies two categories of Emergent Group Characteristics: "Perceptions of" and "Processes." Recalling the significant groupthink challenges presented by ingroup hostility toward outgroups, the basis of the antagonism was centered on an inherent group "morality," which then justified and supported actions against any opposing groups. The advantages of the GGPS-Model are the processes designed to reduce group isolation and potential groupthink by identifying and discussing appropriate "responses to negative feedback, treatment of dissenters, self-censorship and the use of mindguards."

The subsequent and perhaps most important component of the GGPS-Model is identified as the "Decision Process Characteristics." In this regard, the issue of problem identification and the task of engaging in a predecisional information search, survey of objectives, and explicit problem definition risks being unduly influenced by group morality, member unanimity, and attitudes toward opposing groups. The importance of considering alternatives, leading to evaluation and choice, is a critical element of the community decision process in a democratic society, particularly as it relates to the risk of HVE.

3.4.4 General Group Problem-Solving Outcomes

Looking toward community-based risk-reduction strategies for radicalization and HVE, the advantages of the GGPS-Model in response to the contributing components of groupthink are important. GGPS is designed to reduce group isolation, providing appropriate opportunities for debate and even dissent by group members. Group leadership

---

[47]*Ibid.*

decisions using the GGPS-Model provide for decision, political and affective outcomes.

Decision outcomes include acceptance of the decision by those affected by it and/or those who have to implement it, adherence to the decision, implementation success and decision quality. For example, if the leader of the group is not satisfied with the decision, he/she might unilaterally reverse it.

Political outcomes include future motivation of the leader, future motivation of the group and future use of the group. For example, if an outcome does not satisfy the political agenda of the leader, he/she might use the group less or not at all in the future.

Affective outcomes include satisfaction with the leader, satisfaction with the group process and satisfaction with the decision. For example, consensus is achieved regarding the leader, the group and the decision process.

The GGPS-Model offers some insight into a theoretical and practical approach to developing a model that can engage, lead, and monitor a stakeholder group that contributes to community activities and improves the quality of life. While it potentially provides an effective basis for countering the negative outcomes from groupthink decision making, any construct of a moral community rests upon addressing two basic issues: the group and its leadership.

The dangers of group cohesiveness and group insulation, as demonstrated by the CSA example, are apparent. These characteristics discourage dissent, consider fewer alternatives and encourage groupthink. Developing a group dynamic that recognizes the long-term benefits of public diplomacy, focused on understanding the shortcomings of policies intended to counter violent extremism, is the initial step in reducing feelings of group vulnerability and the associated need for self-censorship during the decision-making process. The GGPS-Model offers a potentially effective starting point for faith-based or immigrant groups, which are perhaps already challenged by negative stereotypes, perpetuated by misinformation.

Communities placing a priority on the improvement of their quality of life stand to succeed if collective actions match the group's values or agreed-upon community norms. The stakeholder engagement process begins by inviting analysis and criticism from disparate elements of the group, challenging related safety and security policies. A willingness to openly address grievances related to these government decisions reduces opportunities for opposing groups to exploit perceived or real inconsistent actions. Consensus building is a key element of this process, insomuch as what may appear to be unsolvable problems allows for the consideration of alternative responses that would normally go unnoticed.

A true commitment to democracy requires the fortitude to make hard decisions in the face of emotional adversity. The safety and security quotient are the cornerstones of a community seeking to improve its quality of life, reducing crime generally and the risk of HVE recruitment specifically.

The remaining element in response to the risk of HVE involves addressing group leadership and the importance of impartial, "nondirective" leaders. This component cannot be overstated. "Directive" leaders prone to groupthink have been shown to use less available information, consider fewer alternatives to problems and are prone to mind-guarding, as demonstrated by the evolution of CSA. Unfortunately, these directive leaders, in the interest of expediency, influence the group to acquiesce instead of presenting a diverse collection of viable alternatives. Thus, leadership is critical, and "nondirective" leaders committed to achieving "effective outcomes" stand to point the moral compass of the group in a direction for the good of the community.

The development of an effective model for reducing the risk of radicalization and HVE is complex. While the above discussion offers important insight into how communities might adjust their dynamic and decision-making process to yield more effective risk-reduction, additional work remains. Further theoretical and practical development of these important concepts will necessarily involve scholars and policymakers from a range of disciplines. To more fully address the growing threat of radicalization and HVE, what is needed is focused study and research from all academic arenas and indeed, the development of counterterrorism as a true profession.

FURTHER READING

Ali, A.Y. (2009). *The Meaning of the Holy Qur'an* (11th ed.). Amana Publications, Beltsville, MD.

Aronson, E. (1969). The Theory of Cognitive Dissonance: A Current Perspective. In L. Berkowitz (Ed.) *Advances in Experimental Social Psychology*. Academic Press, New York, NY.

Bakker, E. (2006). *Jihadi Terrorists in Europe: Their Characteristics and the Circumstances in Which They Joined the Jihad: An Exploratory Study*. Netherlands Institute of International Relations Clingendael, The Hague.

Benard, C. (2005). *A Future for the Young, Options for Helping Middle Eastern Youth Escape the Trap of Radicalization*. RAND National Security Research Division, RAND Corporation, Santa Monica, CA.

Bipartisan Policy Center (2011). *Preventing Violent Radicalization in America*. National Security Preparedness Group, Bipartisan Policy Center, Washington, DC.

Bipartisan Policy Center (2012). *Countering Online Radicalization in America*. National Security Program, Homeland Security Project, Bipartisan Policy Center, Washington, DC.

Borum, R. (2011). *Radicalization into violent extremism I: a review of social science theories*. Journal of Strategic Security, 4(4), 7–36.

Brachman, J. (2005). *Global Jihadism: Theory and Practice*. Routledge, London and New York.

Cragin, K. (15 December 2009). *Understanding Terrorist Motivations. Testimony Presented Before the Committee on Homeland Security Subcommittee on Intelligence, Information Sharing and Terrorism Risk Assessment United States House of Representatives*. The RAND Corporation, http://hsc-democrats.house.gov/SiteDocuments/20091215100448-24149.pdf (Retrieved: 12 January 2013).

FBI Records: The Vault. Five Percenters Part 1 of 2. http://vault.fbi.gov/5percent/Five%20Percenters%20Part%201%20of%202/view (Retrieved: 19 January 2013).

Horgan, J. (2005). Psychology of Terrorism. Frank Cass Publishers, London, UK.

Hunter, R. and Heinke, D. (September 2011). *Perspective, Radicalization of Islamist Terrorists in the Western World*. FBI Law Enforcement Bulletin. http://www.fbi.gov/stats-services/publications/law-enforcement-bulletin/september-2011/perspective (Retrieved: 6 January 2013).

Ibish, H. (2010). *Muslim Extremism Stems from Alienation*. The Washington Post. http://onfaith.washingtonpost.com/onfaith/guestvoices/2010/10/muslim_extremism_stems_from_alienation.html (Retrieved: 19 January 2013).

Johnson, C. (4 August 2006). *God, the Black Man and the Five Percenters*. National Public Radio interview, http://www.npr.org/templates/story/story.php?storyId = 5614846 (Retrieved: 19 January 2013).

Kruglanski, A.W. and Fishman, S. (2009). *Psychological Factors in Terrorism and Counterterrorism: Individual, Group, and Organizational Levels of Analysis*. Social Issues and Policy Review, 3,1. http://terpconnect.umd.edu/~ hannahk/Terrorism_files/PsychologicalFactors.pdf (Retrieved: 18 January 2013).

Levin, B. (2003). *Radical Religion in Prison, How Are Prison Officials to Balance Security Interests and the Right of Racial Supremacists to Pursue Religion? The Jury's Still Out*. Southern Poverty Law Center, Intelligence Report. Montgomery, AL, http://www.splcenter.org/get-informed/intelligence-report/browse-all-issues/2003/fall/radical-religion-in-prison (Retrieved: 19 January 2013).

Lorenzo, V. (2010). *Countering Radicalization in America, Lessons from Europe*. United States Institute of Peace, Washington, DC. http://www.usip.org/files/resources/SR262%20-%20Countering_Radicalization_in_America.pdf (Retrieved: 5 January 2013).

Martin, G. (2011). *Terrorism and Homeland Security*. SAGE Publications, Thousand Oaks, CA, p. 4.

McCauley, C. (2009). *Does political radicalization depend on ideology?* Dynamics of Asymmetric Conflict, 2(3), 213–215.

McCauley, C. and Moskalenko, S. (Laurie Fenstermacher ed., 2010). *Individual and Group Mechanisms of Radicalization, in Topical Strategic Multi-Layer Assessment (SMA), Multi-Agency and Air Force Research Laboratory, Multi-Disciplinary White Papers in Support of Counter-Terrorism and Counter-WMD.* http://www.start.umd.edu/start/publications/ U_Counter_Terrorism_White_Paper_Final_January_2010.pdf (Retrieved: 12 January 2013).

Munson, Z. (2008). *The Making of Pro-Life Activists: How Social Movement Mobilization Works.* University of Chicago Press, Chicago, IL.

National Counterterrorism Center (June 2012) *Radicalization Dynamics, A Primer,* Washington, DC .

Patel, F. (2011). *Rethinking Radicalization.* Brennan Center for Justice at New York University School of Law. http://brennan.3cdn.net/f737600b433d98d25e_6pm6beukt.pdf (Retrieved: 6 January 2013).

Pedahzur, A. and Perliger, A. (2006). *The changing nature of suicide attacks—a social network perspective.* Social Forces, 84(4), 1987–2008.

PET (2009). *Radikalisering og terror.* Center for Terroranalyse, Denmark.

Post, J.M., et al. (2003). *The terrorists in their own words: interviews with 35 incarcerated Middle Eastern terrorists.* Terrorism and Political Violence, 15(1), 176.

Post, J.M. (1984). *Notes on a psychodynamic theory of terrorist behavior.* Terrorism: An International Journal, 7(3), 242–256.

Richardson, L. (2006). *What Terrorists Want, Understanding the Enemy, Containing the Threat.* Random House, New York, NY.

Royal Canadian Mounted Police (2009). *Radicalization: A Guide for the Perplexed.* National Security Criminal Investigations, Ottawa, ON.

Sageman, M. (2004). *Understanding Terror Networks.* University of Pennsylvania Press, Philadelphia, PA.

Sageman, M. (2008). *Leaderless Jihad: Terror Networks in the Twenty-First Century.* University of Pennsylvania Press, Philadelphia, PA.

SalafiManhaj.com Research Division (2007). *Is the Salifi Manhaj an Indicator of Terrorism, Political Violence and Radicalisation? A Critical Study of the NYPD Document: Radicalization in the West – The Homegrown Threat, by Mitchell D. Silber and Arvin Bhatt [Senior Intelligence Analysts—NYPD Intelligence Division].* http://www.salafimanhaj.com/pdf/SalafiManhaj_NYPD. pdf (Retrieved: 12 January 2013).

Silber, M.D. and Bhatt, A. (2007). *Radicalization in the West: The Homegrown Threat.* New York Police Department, Intelligence Division, New York, NY.

Stern, J. (2010). *Mind over Martyr how to deradicalize Islamist extremists.* Foreign Affairs, 89, 1, 95–108.

Three Percenter website. About Three Percenter. http://www.threepercenter.org/read.php?4,8 (Retrieved: 19 January 2013).

Travis, A. (20 August 2008). *MI5 report challenges views on terrorism in Britain.* The Guardian. http://www.guardian.co.uk/uk/2008/aug/20/uksecurity.terrorism1 (Retrieved: 6 January 2013).

UK Home Office (2011). *Understanding Vulnerability and Resilience in Individuals to the Influence of Al Qa'ida Violent Extremism, A Rapid Evidence Assessment to Inform Policy and Practice in Preventing Violent Extremism.* Office for Security and Counter-Terrorism. http://www.homeoffice. gov.uk/publications/science-research-statistics/research-statistics/counter-terrorism-statistics/occ98? view = Binary (Retrieved: 20 January 2013).

Leveraging Disciplines Toward a Counterterrorism Profession

Events since the 9/11 terror attacks have demonstrated the dynamic nature of terrorism. Terrorist actors have proven to be adaptive and intelligent in their responses to physical and technological countermeasures. Despite lacking a comprehensive definition, terrorism as a phenomenon can be analyzed through a multitude of academic disciplines. By understanding the scholarly value these disciplines offer, with particular emphasis on the human element, it is possible to explore future interdisciplinary educational approaches to the counterterrorism imperative.

America responded to the 9/11 attacks with military, intelligence and law enforcement. As military action in Afghanistan and Iraq ramped up, the Department of Homeland Security (DHS) was created, representing the nation's largest government reorganization in decades. In addition, there was an interdisciplinary outgrowth of public- and private-sector education and research efforts intended to meet the anticipated demand for security solutions. In one sense, Osama bin Laden created an industry, one that continues to grow.

Terrorism-related study and research in particular is expanding, but is it helping to reduce or contain the risk of another attack? The 2013 bombing of the Boston Marathon could be seen as evidence that homeland security and counterterrorism efforts are lagging behind the threat. Yet, there have been dozens of disrupted plots and attempted attacks revealing that more than a decade of terrorism study and research has not been for naught. Even still, there is always room for improvement.

Facing an ever-present threat, adaptive adversaries, and the increasing risk of HVE recruitment and radicalization, the United States must professionalize counterterrorism as it leverages security tactics, policies, and technology. As an emerging profession, counterterrorism can be examined through the core mission of three broad academic realms: the humanities, the sciences and the social sciences. By considering the focus of each academic area and its methodology of study, it is possible to establish each discipline's value proposition and how these diverse areas might be employed in terrorism research to support a community-based resistance model.

A better understanding of terrorism must come through a multidisciplinary approach, because such a method can better identify research gaps, in turn leading to more comprehensive and effective counterterrorism strategies.[1] Research in the humanities, the sciences and the social sciences overlaps, as do their potential application in response to the threat of terrorism. To prioritize areas most appropriate for future exploration in the development of counterterrorism as a profession, it is important to weigh how each academic foundation applies to existing security challenges, particularly with regard to the unpredictable human element.

4.1 THE HUMANITIES AND COUNTERTERRORISM

The humanities comprise a collection of disciplines devoted to the study of the human condition. The notion of humanity describes the essence of who we are as a rational, creative, intelligent species and the essence of what it means to be human. Humanity encompasses race, gender, and culture, core elements of the human condition that give rise to language, literature, philosophy, religion, art, and by consequence of all of these, history.

As an academic discipline, the humanities engage an "analytical, critical or speculative" approach to the exploration of the human condition. Until recently, study in the humanities was based largely on historical data and research. The increasing availability and importance of digital data, however, provides new opportunities for research efforts, potentially yielding unique and significant contributions to the discipline in the future.

Study of the humanities offers value in part through *critical theory*, first described by Max Horkheimer in of the Frankfurt School of Sociology. According to Horkheimer's 1937 essay, *Traditional and Critical Theory*, critical theory is "oriented toward critiquing and

---

[1]Benard, C. (Ed.) (2005). *A Future for the Young: Options for Helping Middle Eastern Youth Escape the Trap of Radicalization*. RAND Corporation, Santa Monica, CA, WR-354, p. 172. Retrieved from http://www.rand.org/pubs/working_papers/WR-354/.

changing society as a whole, in contrast to traditional theory oriented only to the understanding or explaining it." In either case, the value of much of the research in the humanities aligns with the basic requirements of the scientific method—using theory (critical or traditional) to develop hypotheses, which are in turn tested against facts.

The notion of a "theory" reveals the nexus between the humanities and the terrorism. Examining this concept from the perspective of the adversary, one can assume that through a process of rational decision making, terrorists theorize how best to advance their political objective based on the anticipated consequences of a planned action. This kind of analysis by a defender (e.g., government protective forces or counterterrorism efforts) provides a deeper understanding of HVE as a phenomenon.

The use of a theory, either by the adversary or the defender, reveals a great deal about the actor. Policies, processes and technologies aimed at reducing the threat of terrorism often say more about who *we* are than what we actually propose to achieve. The increasing acceptance of actions that might question the foundations of democratic principles suggests that societies facing increasing threats to their safety and security become more tolerant of aggressive actions. For example, the use of the so-called enhanced interrogation techniques (sometimes called torture) in the pursuit of intelligence in some ways run counter to the principals and mores that have long-guided U.S. respect for human rights and life. Thus, to engage Horkheimer's critical theory model is to consider examining and changing our society as it relates to the threat of terrorism.

Events of the past several decades have shown how terrorist organizations adapt organizationally, operationally and ideologically to changing security approaches. They have moved from hierarchical, top-down traditional command and control structures to decentralized, self-organizing, and resilient designs. Operational schemes employing long and sophisticated planning, surveillance cycles, developed for teams or "cells" with focused training on one target, evolved into solo or "lone-wolf" attackers, encouraged to engage a number of targets as often as possible. The transnational threat of terrorism is evolving to originate less frequently in lawless, economically deprived, remote areas (as seen with core al Qaeda and its affiliates) and is shifting to attacks that are planned and launched in the country of origin (i.e., homegrown).

The 2013 Boston Marathon bombing was followed five weeks later by the murder of a British soldier by a self-proclaimed extremist in the southeast London district of Woolwich. The interesting nexus between these incidents involving Dzhokhar and Tamerlan Tsarnaev in Boston, and Michael Adebowale and Michael Adebolajo in London, are the political motivations behind the attacks. Surviving brother Dzhokhar Tsarnaev, an American citizen and resident of Boston for more than half of his life, cited the U.S. war in Iraq and Afghanistan as cause for the attack. After the fatal hatchet assault on British Drummer Lee Rigby, Abdebowale remained at the scene to be filmed by a witness, declaring the attack was a response to Muslims dying around the world at the behest of Western governments.

The researchable question regarding these and every incident of HVE is associated with identifying their respective radicalization trajectories. The suspects were all homegrown, choosing motivations based on retribution and the notion that Muslims were being victimized as a result of U.S. and UK foreign policy. Inasmuch as these men were largely self-radicalized, however, what were the traumatic events preceding their cognitive openings, making them susceptible to embracing extremist ideologies and choosing to engage in violent action? Could the humanities or other disciplines provide valuable answers?

4.2 THE SCIENCES AND COUNTERTERRORISM

Research in the sciences requires evidence-based methodologies using the scientific method—quantitative knowledge established on observable events or trends with results measured against rigorous re-examination under the same conditions. When applied to the study of terrorism, the scientific method offers an opportunity to research theories associated with pre-incident indicators that suggest behaviors consistent with individuals prone to recruitment and radicalization.

The sciences are concerned with fact. The values of the research community, the researcher, and the sponsoring institution, however, present an opportunity to influence the resulting data, fact or not. It is analogous to a situation where intelligence analysts are given a policy that their intelligence gathering and analysis is intended to support. The policy is driving the intelligence as opposed to the alternative, as the process is designed to work. The ideal research setting is one in which science is unbiased and free of personal values or intent.

The objectivity of science as a bias- and value-free discipline is essential for HVE research. The difference between quantitative and qualitative research does not preclude the researcher's inevitable subjective influence. As a result of the potential for bias, challenges have ensued regarding whether science truly is value-free, raising questions about the impartial nature and authority of the scientific method.[2] Literature in this area supports the fact that there are personal cognitive values that influence scientific research, and "the notion that science is driven exclusively by objectivity in practice and method is not entirely accurate."[3]

The need for unbiased research questions is as important as the scientific method itself. Science-centered research engenders desired outcomes such as testability, reliability, accuracy and exploratory capacities. As science is increasingly engaged and embraced by counterterrorism researchers and practitioners, it could yield reliable knowledge for the consideration of subsequent polices, processes, and technology.

4.3 THE SOCIAL SCIENCES AND COUNTERTERRORISM

The social sciences are devoted to the study of the individual and collective relationships in human society. As an academic discipline, it addresses the related studies of anthropology, economics, history, political science, psychology and sociology. Terrorism generally, and HVE specifically, has the capacity to leverage each of these areas to recruit new adherents, in addition to enhancing their organizational capacity and objectives. At the same time, if political scientists or psychologists are involved in decision making, it could influence the planning process for a government response to an attack on a building.

[2]Allchin, D. (1998). Values in science and in science education. In B.J. Fraser and K.G. Tobin (Eds.), *International Handbook of Science Education*, Vol. 2. Kluwer Academic Publishers, pp. 1083–1092. Retrieved from http://www1.umn.edu/ships/ethics/values.htm.
[3]*Ibid.*

Understanding the important role of a legitimizing ideology is at the core of the risk-reduction challenge. Engaging the social sciences (perhaps even more so than other disciplines) is essential to developing community-based risk-reduction strategies that counter legitimizing ideologies. Using the social sciences to understand extremists' relationships, developed face-to-face or online, is central to generating the appropriate and necessary research questions.

The social sciences apply the scientific method to the study of human behavior and social patterns. Of the aforementioned areas of study, it is psychology that may provide the most critical answers to the issue of recruitment, radicalization, cognitive openings and decisions for violent action. Psychological research has the potential to begin to reveal the social and psychological dimensions of HVE behavior. Research in this area has the capacity to explore some of the previously described critical recruitment elements—such as leadership, group dynamics and cohesion—to explain why some adherents passively support the cause, while others, bent on violent action, become the operational fringe. From a counterterrorism perspective, this research helps frame the question: "What kinds of behaviors are we trying to inhibit?"

Extremist social networks are often complex. Accordingly, the foundational hypothesis for the responding psychological "experiment" is not straightforward. There is a difference between a psychological experiment and experimental psychology. Conducting a psychological experiment requires the scientific method, basing conclusions on empirical evidence. For example, Solomon Asch's aforementioned conformity experiments that demonstrated how the larger group influences an individual's opinions may provide a foundation for understanding extremist group decision making.[4] Experimental psychology uses the scientific method to research the mind and behavior, as demonstrated in the research on "Intertemporal Decision Making," which posits that people prefer immediate smaller rewards over larger rewards delivered later.[5] This work may be instructive as it relates to understanding choice action dynamics of extremist actions. Both of these

---

[4]Asch, S.E. (1951). Effects of group pressure on the modification and distortion of judgments. In H. Guetzkow (Ed.), *Groups, Leadership and Men*. Carnegie Press, Pittsburgh, PA, pp. 177–190. Asch, S.E. (1952). Social Psychology.
[5]Dshemuchadse, M., Scherbaum, S., Goschke, T. (2013). *How decisions emerge: action dynamics in intertemporal decision making*. Journal of Experimental Psychology, 142(1), 93.

methodologies offer value in identifying important behavioral processes that extremist organizations and their leaders consider when determining messages that appeal to their target audiences.

The diversity of terrorists' backgrounds, and the lack of "field" research to support theories of recruitment, radicalization, and disengagement, exacerbate the challenges of responding to this complicated phenomenon. Thus, an improved understanding of social network psychology sets the stage for communities and government to counter the extremist narrative. In this regard, governments will be better positioned to address grievances of marginalized communities that are often the target of extremist messaging.

The post-9/11 era has generated myriad counterterrorism policies, strategies and technology at a hefty price tag. While these endeavors are important, it is just as crucial to quantify their cost-effectiveness. Serious questions regarding actual and measurable detection, deterrence and defense mitigation must be asked to appropriately prioritize future work and investment. Additionally, an improved understanding of the human element will facilitate increased knowledge of extremist engagement, as well as actions to develop community resistance and reduce related risks. Research that gathers and analyzes relevant data using innovative methodologies can inform the implementation of relevant policies and programs.

4.3.1 The Scientific Method and The Study of Terrorists

Since 1994, Marc Sageman has been in the private practice of forensic and clinical psychiatry and has had the opportunity to evaluate approximately 500 murderers. After 9/11, he began collecting biographical material on 400 al Qaeda terrorists to test the validity of the conventional wisdom on terrorism. Sageman argues that much of the international counterterrorism effort and published literature focuses unnecessarily on defining terrorism. Our collective efforts, he says, would be more effectively employed if we focused study on the terrorists themselves. He writes, "the key to unlocking the mysteries surrounding terrorism is found in social science methods — statistics, sampling theory, survey techniques, measurement, and data analysis."[6]

---

[6]Sageman, M. (2008). *Leaderless Jihad, Terror Networks in the Twenty-First Century*. University of Pennsylvania Press, Philadelphia, PA, p. 14.

Some terrorism "experts" have migrated from the field of journalism or intelligence, but they sometimes lack an academic or operational acumen, including the use of social science methodology, the scientific method, and the field experience of managing, investigating, or prosecuting terrorism-related cases. As a result, they may be limited to perfunctory opinions on the subject itself. Their outlooks, usually anecdotal illustrations, merely serve to illustrate, rather than analyze, a specific point. Ultimately, opinions by what may be termed "academic practitioners"—those authorities with years of operational experience and expertise, enhanced by scholarly research—may be the future of counterterrorism as a discipline. Regardless of their professional beginnings, social sciences researchers may be better prepared to ask the "right" questions. Why does a person join a terrorist organization? What do they want to accomplish? Is there an alternative nonviolent strategy? What is their metric for success? Sageman postulates, there are three levels of analysis on which future research should be focused: Micro Analysis (the terrorist), Macro Analysis (the terrorist organization) and Hybrid Analysis (terrorist choices).

4.3.2 Micro Analysis—The Terrorist

For Sageman, the micro-level analysis approach is the most common. The assumption is that behaviors, particularly those associated with decision-making processes, are different in terrorists than in others. When examined by clinical psychologists or psychiatrists, the research question is positioned around determining what is wrong with the individual. This necessarily underscores two assumptions: there is something wrong with the terrorists and the explanation for what went wrong can be found in their background.[7]

From a research perspective, we are left with little in the way of empirical data and supportive evidence by examining terrorists collectively or individually. This fact is exacerbated by two additional challenges: terrorists comprise a small percentage of the general population; and of that small number of terrorists, those who are willing to engage in suicide operations is even less. Although there are some data on membership in terrorist organizations, no one is certain just how large or small these representative groups really are.

[7] *Ibid.* p. 16.

Micro Analysis also focuses on sanity and rationality, which may not be appropriate for understanding terrorists. Criminal behavior assumes some individuals are different from the mainstream population. Sageman explains that this is a rejection of what is called the *null hypothesis*, which posits that a sample is representative of the whole.[8] Psychologists, researchers and counterterrorism officials often suggest a "terrorist personality" that is different from the mainstream and representative of some larger abnormality. Yet, contrary to conventional wisdom, it has been previously illustrated that ordinary people can be motivated to do dreadful things. Thus, terrorism research has yet to reveal a terrorist personality. No study has been able to substantiate that terrorism is a function of an abnormal personality.

While there is merit to understanding how traumatic events can potentially lead to a cognitive opening, we cannot necessarily predict which individuals are predisposed to becoming terrorists. Sageman writes that explanations attributing "bad behaviors to personal disposition while blaming our own on external situations is what social psychologists call the *fundamental error of attribution*."[9] Thus, future research efforts must include an examination of situational factors involved in the recruitment, radicalization and even disengagement continuum to achieve a more holistic, and therefore relevant, study of terrorism.

Finally, Micro Analysis methodology assumes that rational decision-making processes are inherent and that they are used when individuals decide to become terrorists, in some cases killing others and themselves. Yet, individual decision making may become secondary to those of a larger group. Returning to the aforementioned Milgram experiment, a driving factor in the compliance seen in the experiment participants has been described as the *theory of conformism*, which describes the relationship between the group or network and the individual.[10] The theory of conformism explains how the participants, lacking decision-making authority, will leave the decision to the group and its hierarchy. Thus, the group becomes the participant's behavioral model. Social psychology inquiries will be critical to core curriculum for study in the area of terrorism and terrorist behavior.

[8] *Ibid*. p. 17.
[9] *Ibid*. p. 18.
[10] Asch, S. (1955). *Opinions and social pressure*. Scientific American, 193(5), 31–35.

4.3.3 Macro Analysis—The Terrorist Organization

Studies examining the terrorist's environment have yielded expansive sociological explanations for the causes of terrorism. The public would prefer that terrorism, if afforded the same resources and prioritization as other societal ills, would be diminished or eliminated over time. Unfortunately, this will never be the case. We are reminded that we are managing risk, and instances of terrorism are as different as the individuals embracing the concept.

Attempts to profile a terrorist based on socioeconomic factors, religion, education, economic opportunities or susceptibility to seductive sermons offered by charismatic leaders has yielded one result—there is no profile. From a macro level, radicalization causalities are linked with traditional organizational command and control constructs as factors that encourage individuals to become terrorists. In other words, individuals enter the group dynamic at the lower echelon and over time are provided guidance and instruction designed to increase their loyalty and engagement. Interesting questions result from this process. What kind of social or group structure facilitates or encourages terrorism? If the same factors (social, economic, political or cultural) impact millions of people, why do so few become terrorists?[11] Is this an issue of *specificity*? If so, what is it that is so unique about terrorists that causes these factors to motivate violent extremism?

There are societies that have developed a resistance to terrorist influences because of a deterrence quotient that psychologically empowers its constituents. The lethality of a bombing incident on Jaffa Street in Israel in 2012 was significantly minimized by the actions of a bystander. The citizen observed an unattended bag at a bus stop and rather than notifying the authorities, he demanded people nearby to evacuate the area. The bomb was remotely detonated as the bus arrived, killing one person; however, many more would have died had the citizen failed to take charge. Israel's community norm of taking care of each other, and the practice that everyone is a first responder, is at the core of its terrorism-resistant culture.

All research examinations require contemplation of terrorism's root cause. Extremism is always a factor of terrorist behavior. Although extremism (particularly political extremism) is a radical expression of

---

[11]See footnote 6, p. 21.

political values characterized by opposing views or interests, it is not always accompanied by violence, revolution, or transnational goals. Inasmuch as it is such an important element of terrorist engagement, central research questions are: How does groupthink engage? How do individuals form a cell, willing to fit into a literal or virtual organizational structure, awaiting orders outlining the next attack? In other words, what is the root cause of radicalization?

We are presented with two challenging research inquiries: identifying the societal influences leading to terrorism and investigating the road to radicalization, which is eventually shared by a group. Although appealing endeavors, the low frequency of terrorist incidents exacerbates the research challenge. Terrorism is not a constant phenomenon. The ebb and flow of terrorist incidents fails to provide adequate information to determine how terrorists evaluate their milieu and develop the need and means to explore alternative actions, some of which are violent.

4.3.4 Hybrid Analysis—Terrorist Choices

The micro and macro approaches fail to provide the necessary analysis for a comprehensive research outcome. A hybrid of these two methodologies, however, may be a better tool for understanding the human element. A hybrid approach can focus on what terrorists have in common with regard to recruitment, social network composition, familial affiliation, and first encounters with the ideology. As some terrorist organizations have evolved into a more decentralized, bottom-up structure, the hybrid research design would take the same approach in an attempt to better understand the actors who comprise the organization and its actions.

A hybrid approach focuses on the terrorist pathway with respect to "pre-radicalization", recruitment, indoctrination, violent action and even disengagement, asking: "Why do people become terrorists; if not, why not?" These are complex questions insomuch as terrorist groups and their respective ideologies are vastly different. From a collective viewpoint, terrorist groups, particularly operational cells, maintain a tight social network. Operational security and the development of trust require a bond that facilitates their ability to function as an effective unit. Examples such as the terrorists responsible for the 2004 Madrid train bombings and the 2005 London attacks, who all knew one another over a lifetime, having grown up and attended the same school, provided a certain level of trust and mutual respect. Natural groups such as these, under the influence of groupthink socialization and conformism, would explain their collective radicalization pathway.

Although the hybrid approach would seem intuitive toward an understanding of how homegrown groups create their collective identity, Sageman cautions: "There is no academic discipline that has conducted comprehensive studies of natural groups, as opposed to groups of strangers that can be manipulated experimentally."

The discipline and science of counterterrorism lacks data, an essential element if the scientific method is to be applied. It is rare that experts talk to, investigate, prosecute or visit with a terrorist in their natural environment—their community. Personal experience and expertise dictates that the researcher has to engage on an individual, communal and organizational level with terrorists if the inquiry is to be valid. This is a difficult proposition, as due to the personal and national security issues associated with such interactions with terrorists, opportunities for experts to conduct direct research are few and far between. Obtaining data presents a formidable task.

4.4 SOCIAL NETWORK CHARACTERISTICS

As stated previously, terrorist organizations, particularly al Qaeda, have demonstrated extraordinary organizational adaptability in the face of adversity. The evolution from a hierarchical, top-down structure to one that is essentially "leaderless" is explained in Sageman's exhaustive study on the issue. His work challenges conventional wisdom about terrorism, observing that the key to mounting an effective counterstrategy against future attacks requires a thorough understanding of the networks that allow these new terrorists to exist.

Terrorist networks are resilient, due in large part to their dynamic capacity to evolve and adapt. Examples such as the terrorist tactical responses to security countermeasures in the aviation domain (concealing explosives in shoes, undergarments on commercial flights and choosing to target cargo aircraft), or messaging techniques using chat rooms and other online resources, clearly demonstrate terrorist networks' innovative capacity. Although these tactical improvements are noteworthy, messaging is the heartbeat of their survival and growth. Extremist ideologies associated with terrorism and HVE can be propelled through social networking. In that regard, the evolution of social networking has the potential to enable one central character. Al Qaeda senior recruiter and operational planner Anwar al-Awlaki's network is a case in point.

Al-Awlaki was a spiritual advisor for terrorists Nawaf al-Hazmi and Khalid al-Mihdhar while they were in San Diego training for the "Planes Operation." This was to become the plan for the 9/11 attacks. After the attack, al-Awlaki became an extraordinary recruiter, leveraging the hyper-connectivity of our modern society via the Internet.[12] His ability to coach and inspire other would-be terrorists is evidenced in incidents occurring 8 years after the 9/11 attacks.

September 24, 2009—Michael Finton, also known as Talib Islam, attempted to bomb the Paul Findley Federal Building and the nearby offices of Congressman Aaron Schock in Springfield, Illinois.

November 5, 2009—Major Nidal Hasan was the sole suspect in a mass shooting at Fort Hood in Texas, killing 13 people and wounding 29 others.

December 25, 2009—Umar Farouk Abdulmutallab, also known as "the Underwear Bomber," attempted to detonate an improvised explosive device concealed in his underwear aboard Northwest Airlines Flight 253 en route from Amsterdam to Detroit.

April 2010—Zachary Adam Chesser, also known as Abu Talhah al-Amrikee, posted a warning to the creators of the television show *South Park*, threatening to kill them for depicting the prophet Muhammad in the 200th episode. He was arrested 3 months later for aiding al-Shabaab, an affiliate of al Qaeda.

May 14, 2010—Roshana Choudhry stabbed British politician Stephen Creswell Timms as punishment for voting to support the Iraq War and as revenge for the Iraqi people.

June 5, 2010—Omar Eduardo Almonte and Mohamed Alessa were arrested at JFK Airport as they attempted to board flights to travel from Egypt to Somalia to join al-Shabaab with the stated intent to kill American troops.

---

[12]Bipartisan Policy Center (December 2012). *Countering Online Radicalization in America.* National Security Program, Homeland Security Project.

All of these individuals, some of them Americans, had one thing in common—they were influenced by online sermons delivered by Anwar al-Awlaki. This group may be viewed as a network or connected *nodes*. As described by Sageman, "Some nodes are more popular and are attached to more links, connecting them to more isolated nodes. These more connected nodes, called *hubs*, are important components of the terrorist network."[13]

From an organizational perspective, the individuals in al-Awlaki's network represent nodes, and al-Awlaki himself served as a hub in the al Qaeda hierarchy. This represents what is defined as a *small world network*. Sageman suggests, it is the "robustness of the network" that may provide insight regarding research efforts to contain or reduce the threat of terrorism. Using al-Awlaki's example, removing him from the network provides the potential for the nodes to become disconnected, reducing their capability to organize a sophisticated attack. Lacking a hub, the nodes would be reduced to autonomous operations, often by lone actors. Al-Awlaki's role was critical, as he served as the communications center for the system, particularly as it related to ideological guidance and motivation for violent action.

4.5 THE COMMUNITY NEXUS

Evidence-based research is critical to leveraging academic disciplines in support of effective policies that will encourage communities to engage in a culture of cooperation. As this research and empirical data is generally lacking, HVE responses will continue to be considered and implemented based on biased and sometimes politicized information. This misinformation affects the very communities needed for engagement and risks their marginalization, possibly fueling a negative sentiment toward the identified population. As residents perceive government bias based on insensitive policies, programs or rhetoric, the foundation for personal or group grievances is developed, potentially creating a cognitive opening for radicalization. The necessary data to help inform risk-reduction strategies will only result from communities that are empowered to engage and define the problem set.

---

[13]Sageman, M. (2004). *Understanding Terror Networks*. University of Pennsylvania Press, Philadelphia, PA, p. 137.

It is critically important that we examine a diversity of environments that lead to HVE. Understanding the complexities of HVE is an education and awareness process that should be shared with the intended community and stakeholders (e.g., community members, researchers, government representatives, private organizations). Inasmuch as any community may have an individual or a group with the potential to consider or engage in HVE, there is no "target" population. Communities engaged and committed to improving their quality of life, prioritizing safety and security, serve as much as a potential test population as those neighborhoods lacking cohesion or leadership. The "Green Bay Way,"[14] implemented in Green Bay, Wisconsin, in 1995, is considered a best practice for Community Oriented Policing (COP). The COP program places officers on foot in the neighborhood in an effort to develop a relationship with the community and reduce crime. The Green Bay Way developed successful community partnerships, resulting in private-sector funding for a variety of innovative programs. Conversely, despite continuing efforts for an effective COP program, Wilmington, Delaware, has fared far worse. While Delaware overall ranked moderately well in the peace index (which looked at factors such as police per capita), Wilmington earned the number one spot[15] for highest rate of violent crimes per 100,000 people in 2012. In either case, the repeated need for comparative data is critical, as is the ability to use basic inquiries associated with the humanities, sciences and social sciences in a manner that "shares" the process with the stakeholders.

Communities have become particularly sensitive to grant-funded research efforts, complaining of researchers' lack of sustained interest or participation at the end of a funding cycle. They abhor feeling like nothing more than subjects in an "experiment." Additionally, assumptions are made that disadvantaged communities, with the day-to-day challenges they may face due to poverty, unemployment and crime, are not interested in something as specific as HVE. Finally, introducing a study pronouncing a myopic focus on HVE, failing to consider "nuisance" activities (e.g., graffiti, loitering, trash, etc.) as having a higher priority

[14]Arts, J. (1995). *Best Practices in Community Oriented Policing. The "Green Bay Way."* http://www.innovativepolicing.com/files/Best%20Practices%20in%20Community%20Policing.pdf (Retrieved: 27 June 2013).
[15]*Top Ten Most Dangerous Cities in America.* Parenting Magazine. http://www.parenting.com/gallery/most-dangerous-cities-in-america-2012 (Retrieved: 27 June 2013).

to local residents, may create an initial relationship disconnect that is deemed irrevocable. These communities seek general public safety (as any community would), and the sciences can provide research vehicles to facilitate the initial conversation, if broached intelligently.

The essence of the study of the humanities as an engagement in critical theory, orientated toward critiquing and changing society as a whole, lends itself to a beginning dialogue regarding the ills of the community partnered in the effort. Well-intended government programs (such as the U.K.'s Prevent Program, discussed in the next chapter) that are developed without stakeholder input on the challenges, scope and potential impact of the program, may face resistance and rejection. Research studies are no different, often enlisting idealistic and naïve researchers who lack any insight about the environment and demonstrate behaviors that confirm they are on a data-gathering quest, leading subjects to perceive that personal relationships are not important or quantifiable components of the study. Critically, it is the relationships that will yield the baseline information that identifies the challenges that need to be targeted for community change.

Engagement in sciences and social sciences research provides for community opportunities to assist in the identification of knowledge gaps related to HVE pathways. Questions associated with social factors regarding who becomes involved, psychological considerations for why people become involved, and the situational elements regarding how people become engaged can only be informed by individuals, groups, and the community. Understanding that the radicalization pathways may be as individual as the people themselves, every piece of information provides another element of critical data. These data are essential if the study of HVE is to be served by the application of the scientific method.

Community-based, risk-reduction designs targeting HVE cannot be identified, discussed or considered for implementation without the affected community's involvement in problem identification. The examination of the human element and social network characteristics regarding individual and collective relationships in human society are best served by social sciences engagement. As the radicalization pathway is a multi-step process, so too is the effort to identify strategies to reduce or contain the threat. There is no one-size-fits-all strategy. The identification of community characteristics determined to be more resistant to extremist ideologies should be challenged to withstand academic and scientific rigor, if they are to be deemed valid and potentially worthy of replication and "best-practice" consideration.

With these considerations and approaches in mind, it is possible to begin developing a model for community engagement and risk reduction. While no model can be applied wholesale to every potentially threatened community, there are some core elements that can prove essential in the focused effort to interrupt the radicalization pathway and reduce the risk of HVE.

FURTHER READING

Abuza, Z. (2009). The disengagement and rehabilitation of Jemaah Islamiyah detainees in Southeast Asia: a preliminary assessment. In T. Bjørgo and J. Horgan (Eds.), *Leaving Terrorism Behind: Disengagement from Political Violence*. Routledge, New York, NY.

Allchin, D. (1998). Values in science and in science education. In B.J. Fraser and K.G. Tobin (Eds.), *International Handbook of Science Education* (2, pp. 1083–1092). Kluwer Academic Publishers, Norwell, MA.

Ashour, O. (November 5, 2008). *De-radicalization of jihad? The impact of Egyptian Islamic revolutionists on Al Qaeda*. Perspectives on Terrorism, 11, 14.

Ashour, O. (2009). *The Deradicalization of Jihadists: Transforming Armed Islamist Movements*. Routledge, New York and London.

Asch, S. (1955). *Opinions and social pressure*. Scientific American, 193(5), 31–35.

Bakker, E. (December 2006). *Terrorists in Europe*. Netherlands Institute of International Relations, Clingendael, the Netherlands, Retrieved from http://www.clingendael.nl/publications/2006/20061200_cscp_csp_bakker.pdf.

Bandura, A. (1998). Mechanisms of moral disengagement. In Walter Reich (Ed.) *Origins of Terrorism: Psychologies, Ideologies, Theologies, States of Mind*. Woodrow Wilson Center Press, Washington, DC.

Barabasi, A. (2003). *Linked—How Everything Is Connected to Everything Else and What It Means for Business, Science, and Everyday Life*. Penguin Group, London.

Barrett, R. and Bokhari, L. (2009). Deradicalization and rehabilitation programmes targeting religious terrorists and extremists in the Muslim world: an overview. In T. Bjørgo and J. Horgan (Eds.), *Leaving Terrorism Behind: Disengagement from Political Violence*. Routledge, New York, NY.

Benard, C. (Ed.) (2005). *A Future for the Young: Options for Helping Middle Eastern Youth Escape the Trap of Radicalization* RAND Corporation, Santa Monica, CAWR-354. Retrieved from http://www.rand.org/pubs/working_papers/WR-354/.

Bjorgo, T. (2005). Reducing recruitment and promoting disengagement from extremist groups: the case of racist sub-cultures. In C. Benard (Ed.) *A Future for the Young: Options for Helping Middle Eastern Youth Escape the Trap of Radicalization*. RAND Corporation, Santa Monica, CAWR-354. Retrieved from http://www.rand.org/pubs/working_papers/WR-354/.

Boucek, C. (September 2008). *Saudi Arabia's "Soft" Counterterrorism Strategy: Prevention, Rehabilitation, and Aftercare*. Carnegie Papers, 97, Carnegie Endowment for International Peace. Washington, DC. Retrieved from http://carnegieendowment.org/files/cp97_boucek_saudi_final.pdf.

Boucek, C. (2009). Extremist re-education and rehabilitation in Saudi Arabia. In T. Bjørgo and J. Horgan (Eds.), *Leaving Terrorism Behind: Disengagement from Political Violence*. Routledge, New York, NY.

Boucek, C. Beg, S. and Horgan, J. (2009). Opening the jihadi debate: Yemen's Committee for Dialogue. In T. Bjørgo and J. Horgan (Eds.), *Leaving Terrorism Behind:* Disengagement from Political Violence. Routledge, New York, NY.

Bubalo, A. (10 June 2008). *Sageman vs. Hoffman: The New War of Ideas*. The Interpreter, Lowy Institute for International Policy. Retrieved from http://www.lowyinterpreter.org/post/2008/06/10/Sageman-vs-Hoffman-The-new-war-of-ideas.aspx?p = true.

Carroll, J. (Spring 2011). "Laws of Nature," *The Stanford Encyclopedia of Philosophy*. Edward N. Zalta (Ed.). Retrieved from http://plato.stanford.edu/archives/spr2011/entries/laws-of-nature/.

Cragin, K., Chalk, P., Grant, A., Helmus, T.C., et al. (2006). *Curbing Militant Recruitment in Southeast Asia*. RAND Corporation, Santa Monica, CA, unpublished.

Crenshaw, A. (2007). *Understanding Terrorist Innovation*. Routledge, London.

Deutsche Presse Agentur (August 24, 2009) [German Press Agency], "Ausstieg fur islamistische Extremisten schwer" [Exit difficult for Islamic extremists].

Ebaugh, H. (1988). *Becoming an Ex: The Process of Role Exit*. University of Chicago Press, Chicago, IL.

Garfinkel, R. (April 2007). *Personal Transformations: Moving from Violence to Peace*. Volume 31. United States Institute of Peace Special Report 186. Washington, DC.

Harding, S. (1991). *Whose Science? Whose Knowledge?* Cornell University Press, New York, NY.

Hegghammer, T. (2006). *Terrorist recruitment and radicalization in Saudi Arabia*. Middle East Policy Council, 13(4), 39−60.

Horgan, J. (2005). *The Psychology of Terrorism*. Routledge, London.

Horgan, J. (2008). *Deradicalization or Disengagement?* Perspectives on Terrorism, 2(4).

Horgan, J. (2009). Individual disengagement: a psychological analysis. In T. Bjørgo and J. Horgan (Eds.), *Leaving Terrorism Behind:* Disengagement from Political Violence. Routledge, New York, NY.

Horkheimer, M. (1937). *Traditional and Critical Theory*. Translated by Matthew J. O'Connell. Retrieved from: http://www.slashdocs.com/kpxzqx/horkheimer-traditional-and-critical-theory-1937.html.

Ilich, I. (1971). Deschooling Society. Retrieved from http://www.ecotopia.com/webpress/deschooling.htm.

Internet Encyclopedia of Philosophy (IEP), A Peer-Reviewed Academic Resource. *Laws of Nature*. Retrieved from http://www.iep.utm.edu/lawofnat/#H1.

Jackson, B. (2001). *Technology acquisition by terrorist groups*. Studies in Conflict and Terrorism, 24, 3.

Kellner, D. *Critical Theory and the Crisis of Social Theory*. Illuminations. Retrieved from http://www.uta.edu/huma/illuminations/kell5.htm.

Lum, C. Kennedy, L. (Eds.) (2012) *Evidence-Based Counterterrorism Policy*. Springer Series on Evidence-Based Crime Policy, Vol. 3.

Martin, G. (2011). Terrorism and Homeland Security. SAGE Publications, Inc. Thousands Oaks, CA.

McCauley, C. and Moskalenko, S. (2008). *Mechanisms of political radicalization: pathways toward terrorism*. Terrorism and Political Violence, 20, 415−433.

Milgram, S. (1974). *Obedience to Authority; An Experimental View*. HarperCollins Publishers, New York, NY.

Morris, M., Eberhard, F., Rivera, J. and Watsula, M. (May 2010). *Deradicalization: A Review of the Literature with Comparison to Findings in the Literatures on Deganging and Deprogramming*. Institute for Homeland Security Solutions, Durham, NC.

Nesser, P. (2005). Profiles of jihadist terrorists in Europe. In C. Benard (Ed.) *A Future for the Young: Options for Helping Middle Eastern Youth Escape the Trap of Radicalization*. RAND Corporation, Santa Monica, CA WR-354. Retrieved from http://www.rand.org/pubs/working_papers/WR354/.

Noricks, D. (2009). Disengagement and deradicalization: processes and programs. In P.K. Davis and K. Cragin (Eds.), *Social Sciences for Counterterrorism: Putting the Pieces Together*. RAND Corporation, Santa Monica, CA Retrieved from http://www.rand.org/pubs/monographs/2009/RAND_MG849.pdf.

Rubin, E. (March 7, 2004) *The Jihadi Who Kept Asking Why*. New York Times. Retrieved from http://www.nytimes.com/2004/03/07/magazine/the-jihadi-who-kept-asking-why.html?pagewanted = 1.

Sageman, M. (2004). *Understanding Terror Networks*. University of Pennsylvania Press, Philadelphia, PA.

Sageman, M. (2008). *Leaderless Jihad, Terror Networks in the Twenty-First Century*. University of Pennsylvania Press, Philadelphia, PA.

Stern, J. (2003). *Terror in the Name of God, Why Religious Militants Kill*. Harper-Collins, New York, NY.

Stern, J. (2010). Mind over martyr: How to deradicalize Islamist extremists. *Foreign Affairs*, 89,1, pp. 95–108. January/February.

Weinberg, L. (June 2008). *Two Neglected Areas of Terrorism Research: Careers after Terrorism and How Terrorists Innovate*. Perspectives of Terrorism, pp. 11–18. http://www.terrorismanalysts.com/pt/index.php/pot/article/view/49/101.

Wimsatt, W.C. (1981). Robustness, reliability and overdetermination. In M. Brewer and B. Collins (Eds.), *Scientific Inquiry and the Social Sciences*. Jossey-Bass, San Francisco, CA, pp. 124–163.

CHAPTER 5

A Mosaic of Engagement

Homegrown violent extremists all have families and live in communities that, complicit or not, possess the potential to reduce the risk of a deadly attack. With an appreciation of how charismatic figures, group dynamics and the radicalization pathway contribute to the emergence of HVE, it is essential to understand and leverage a community's identified priorities as a means to enhance public safety. Doing so requires a new kind of community-based strategy. Presented here is such a model: *Mosaic of Engagement*.

The goal of the *Mosaic of Engagement* model is to challenge and contain violent extremism and radicalization, and to reduce the threat to local public safety and national security. Although some community oriented policing (COP) models have been successful, the *Mosaic* approach holds all of the stakeholders as equal partners. It is a model developed on decades of research and professional practice addressing the issues of street gangs and terrorism. The resulting phases leverage best practices and introduce critical activities missing from similar efforts. Much of this work can be done in schools, focused on grades Kindergarten through 12 (K−12). Efforts to reduce the risk of HVE are best accomplished when incorporated into the public safety framework, employing existing programs that address crime and violence while safeguarding children and the overall community.

The concept of a *Mosaic* program draws in part from the United Kingdom's Preventing Violent Extremism Strategy (*Prevent*), considered one of the best in the world when it was implemented in 2003. Yet, the program did have its shortcomings. It was perceived to have a negative impact on Muslim communities, as they were the only communities identified as being at risk for HVE recruitment and radicalization. Given what has already been established about the nature of HVE (that it cuts across numerous motivating factors, religions and ethnicities), for such a program to be effective in the United States, it necessarily requires expanding the scope while endorsing a clearer methodology for identifying risk.

In addition to public perception, *Prevent* was limited in the evaluation process and was challenged to measure prevention. Measuring crime prevention generally, and HVE recruitment and radicalization specifically, is vitally important to determine a program's efficiency and effectiveness vis-à-vis costs and benefits. For future programs such as *Mosaic*, evaluation standards and principles must be in place, not just to provide evidence of the effectiveness of a program but also to prevent the kind of narrow community focus seen in the U.K. program.

Despite its shortcomings, between 2005 and 2010, *Prevent* became the most widely imitated counter-radicalization strategy. Similar programs were used in Denmark, Australia and Canada, with Germany and Sweden incorporating some aspects in their respective counterterrorism policies.[1] Because *Prevent* was the prototype and catalyst for programs that use the community engagement approach to disrupting the radicalization pathway, the U.K. program offers a rare case study that can reveal how a similar community-based framework might be implemented in the United States. In that regard, we look specifically at leveraging the successful "community indicators" model implemented in City Heights, San Diego, regarding the applicability and effectiveness of *Mosaic*.

5.1 A U.K. MODEL

In an effort to reduce the risk of "al Qaeda-inspired" recruitment, radicalization, and related terrorist incidents in the aftermath of numerous attempted and successful attacks in the United States, Europe, and around the world, the United Kingdom launched the *Prevent* strategy. At its core, *Prevent* focused on radicalization and recruitment prevention (rather than simply HVE detection) and acknowledged the importance of enlisting the community in the fight against terrorism. In the words of Charles Farr, the head of the U.K.'s Office for Security and Counter-terrorism, *Prevent* "was the Government's recognition that as a nation, we cannot arrest our way out of the terrorist threat we face" nor can we "protect ourselves physically to the point where the threat is mitigated entirely."[2]

---

[1]Bipartisan Policy Center (2011). *Preventing Violent Radicalization in America*. National Security Preparedness Group, p. 21.

[2]Farr, C. (19 January 2010). *Communities and Local Government Committee: Evidence.*

Before the turn of the century, al Qaeda's U.K. media network broadcast rhetoric that emphasized, in extremist terms, the supposed inherent conflict between Islam and the West.[3] In 1996 and 1998, Osama bin Laden gave interviews to the London-based *Al Quds al-Arabia* newspaper, announcing his so-called fatwas, declaring war on Zionists and Western crusaders.[4]

After the 9/11 attacks, this kind of message in the public forum became that much more prevalent, with increasingly vocal (and thereby visible) extremist preachers referencing oppressive conditions suffered by Bosnian Muslims or subjugation in Algeria and Chechnya. These and other increases in activism swirled into a perfect storm, fueled further by the U.K.'s invasion of Iraq in 2003. British extremists plotted attacks within the country and actually traveled to the region to fight the Coalition Forces. The U.K. Government realized the importance of working from within their country and from the ground up, which led to *Prevent*.

While an innovative and insightful approach to the growing potential for HVE in the United Kingdom, the initial strategy was criticized for four primary problems:

1. *The strategy's concept of radicalization*: There was a lack of consensus or conceptual clarity on the definition of radicalization. As already discussed, there is no consistent definition of what radicalization means. In the case of *Prevent*, the potential for HVE was defined exclusively by religious affiliation.
2. *A narrow focus on Muslims*: The original program looked exclusively at the Muslim community. This revealed flawed assumptions, foremost that only Muslims in the United Kingdom had the potential to engage in HVE. This labeled all Muslims as potentially "at-risk" while ignoring other groups engaged in extremist activities.
3. *The implementation methodology*: The program funded efforts in Muslim communities based on the size of the Muslim population in a given area. Inasmuch as the additional risk factors[5] were ignored

---

[3]Nacos, B.L. (2007). *Al-Qaeda's Propaganda Advantage and How to Counter It*. Perspectives on Terrorism, 1(4).

[4]Omand, Sir David (2012). *The Terrorist Threat to the UK in the Post-9/11 Decade*. Journal of Terrorism Research, 3(1).

[5]Kundani, A. (2007). *Spooked. Preventing Violent Extremism—Winning Hearts and Minds*, pp. 12–14.

(particularly other domestic sources of extremism), the community perceived that the program was intended to "spy on Muslims."[6]
4. *Negative program consequences*: In considering the Muslim population as a unified community and viewing all Muslims as suspect (irrespective of behavior), the program inadvertently created a relationship of mistrust. This compromised the goal of community engagement and support and potentially helped create an environment ripe for extremist recruitment based on resentment of the British government.

In response to the flaws of the original program, *Prevent* was reviewed in 2011 by the U.K. Government's Home Secretary, minister in charge of the Home Office, which is responsible for immigration, security and law enforcement. A comprehensive set of data collection methods was employed, including consultation events, focus groups and an online questionnaire. This came in addition to a 2010 House of Commons Communities and Local Government Select Committee report, *Preventing Violent Extremism*, which found that the focus on the Muslim community had been unhelpful, stigmatizing, and alienating and could be perceived as legitimizing the extreme right. It also found that resource allocation was not based on risk. Overall, the review determined that the program "confused the delivery of Government policy to promote integration with Government policy to prevent terrorism."[7]

The strategy was revised following this review, and the amended program seeks to:

• Respond to the ideological challenge of terrorism and aspects of extremism, and the threat faced from those who promote these views.
• Provide practical help to prevent people from being drawn into terrorism and ensure they are given appropriate advice and support.
• Work with a wide range of sectors where there are risks of radicalization, employing tactics via education, criminal justice, faith, charities, the Internet and health.[8]

---

[6]Dodd, V. (2009). *Government anti-terrorism strategy "spies" on innocent*. Guardian.
[7]Council on Foreign Relations (2011). *UK Counterterrorism Strategy, 2011*.
[8]Home Office website. *Prevent strategy 2011*.

These are important improvements that, when paired with an understanding of the initial failings, offer powerful lessons for the development of a U.S.-specific community engagement program to prevent HVE.

5.2 A U.S. MODEL

As discussed, HVE can arise from myriad ideologies, grievances and communities. Changing demographics in City Heights, San Diego, indicate a growing propensity for radicalization and recruitment in the area due to an influx of residents from challenged African and Asian nations and the existing Latino gang situation. Indeed, there are already examples emerging from the community that show the threat is real. In 2013, four residents of City Heights were found guilty of supporting the terrorist group al-Shabaab.[9]

Located in the eastern part of San Diego, California, City Heights' strength and potential weakness is its ethnic diversity. City Heights is a business and residential area, including 16 distinct, densely populated neighborhoods: Corridor, Teralta West, Teralta East Colima Park, Cherokee Point, Castle, Fairmont Village, Fox Canyon, Chollas Creek, Azalea Park, Swan Canyon, Islenair (a city-designated historic district), Hollywood Park, Ridgeview, Fairmount Park and Bayridge.

City Heights is one of the most ethnically diverse areas of the country, including both native-born and immigrant residents. More than 40% have immigrated from Latin America, Asia, and Africa, with many of these residents being newly arrived and some from failing states.[10] Only 63% of adults have a high school diploma, 33% are not fluent in English and 27% live in poverty.[11] In 2009, the household median income was $26,232, with 28% of all households earning less than $15,000 and another 30% earning between $15,000 and $29,999 a year. In short, nearly half of the community is made up of immigrants from troubled lands, facing new social and economic challenges to finding success in America.

---

[9]Brumfield, B. (23 February 2013). *Four Somalis in U.S. found guilty of supporting terrorists back home.* CNN U.S.
[10]Price Charities website. http://www.pricecharities.com/City-Heights-Initiative/.
[11]*Ibid.*

City Heights is an older neighborhood, and for a time, crime was on the rise. The economy suffered, and the area was all but abandoned. In 1993, however, Sol Price, founder of Price Club and FedMart, spearheaded redevelopment projects via a Smart Growth strategy implemented by the City of San Diego.[12] The projects attempted to enhance the quality of life by leveraging community diversity and engagement to address crime, education, urban development, and economic improvements.

5.3 A SAFETY INITIATIVE AS A PRELUDE TO A *MOSAIC OF ENGAGEMENT*

Created in January 2012, the City Heights Safety Initiative was the product of a joint effort between Price Charities (a public nonprofit), Price Family Charitable Fund (a private family foundation), and the City Heights community. Led by the Consensus Organizing Center at San Diego State University, the initiative is focused on reducing crime and helping people feel safe in their neighborhoods.[13] To implement the initiative, the city employed the charities as *tipping point connectors*. (i.e., "strategically located people who are committed, competent and connected.")

This is representative of a "community indicators" model, which empowers nonprofit organizations in the community to measure quality-of-life outcomes through self-organized efforts, leveraging existing partnerships between nonprofit, government and business coalitions. This is a particularly effective approach, as it reduces the concerns of bias or politicized outcomes expressed during the discussion of science-based research. Simply put, programs deemed unsuccessful will cease to be funded. For example, evaluators claiming reduced homicide rates, while violent and property crimes increase, offer a skewed illustration of programmatic success. The opportunity for policy makers to highlight desired outcomes while failing to present the entire picture is reduced as a result of this holistic community approach.

At the outset, the program's leadership met with stakeholders to prepare for the 2-year process. A series of meetings included

---

[12]Author is an adjunct professor in the Sol Price School of Public Policy at the University of Southern California.
[13]City Heights Safety Initiative website.

community representatives, law enforcement, academics, policy makers, and leaders from across different sectors in large and small groups. This collective effort led to the initiative's comprehensive framework. Initially, stakeholders organized into four groups to identify and prioritize safety issues and develop a strategic plan of action.

To prioritize community needs, the project groups engaged processes of asset mapping, resident interviews, safety audits and crime statistics analysis. After 2 months, the groups shared their findings, and it was clear that while crime and gang violence were a concern, the community's more salient problems were largely "nuisance" issues, such as the need for trash cans, skate parks and crosswalks.[14]

The intermediate outcomes yielded Crime Prevention Through Environmental Design (CPTED) recommended solutions. CPTED is an interdisciplinary approach to public safety and deterring criminal behavior through environmental design. The design is intended to influence adversarial decisions preceding criminal acts.[15]

Returning to the challenge of transitioning *Prevent* to a U.S.-specific *Mosaic* strategy, the importance of the kind of commitment seen in City Heights cannot be overstated. Engaging residents to identify and determine problem areas is an essential first step to any effective program. One major failing in counterterrorism-focused efforts is the omission of relationship building and the importance of quality-of-life issues. These factors drive the public safety discussion, and they are the foundation of community conversations about HVE. When stakeholders can agree that public safety is an essential element in the community's quality of life, that consensus provides the best opportunity for reducing the risk of violent extremism recruitment and radicalization. These activities put a "human face" on the personal community experiences and information to be used as data. Additionally, consensus facilitates an informed civil discourse, revealing shared civic goals.

---

[14]This kind of outcome is reminiscent of the "Broken Windows Theory," a theory introduced in a 1982 article by social scientists George L. Kelling and James Q. Wilson, proposing that efforts to monitor and improve urban environments may further stop vandalism and the potential for other more serious crime.

[15]This process is intended to reduce the presence of obtrusive physical security barriers, such as barricades, fencing topped with razor ribbon and intimidating signage, by using items such as trees, line-of-sight open spaces and vehicular traffic flow designs to discourage the would-be offender while also enhancing public safety.

5.4 EXERTING POSITIVE INFLUENCE ON THE ENVIRONMENT

As noted, terrorism is the product of an alienated individual, a legitimizing ideology and an enabling environment. The environment (i.e., the community) is most susceptible to positive influence to reduce the risk of HVE. The issue of the enabling environment must be addressed in terms of enhancing social morality, responsibility, and community integrity, with the intended outcome of facilitating community-based efforts to identify and explore solutions to the continuing challenges.

Many motivations for propelling an individual through the radicalization pathway toward HVE are associated with grievances, such as conflicted identity, injustice, oppression or socioeconomic exclusion. These are all likely hurdles faced by immigrants to a new society, such as those in City Heights. Yet, each community encounters circumstances unique to their demographic, citizen makeup and other characteristics. As well as understanding how grievances can lead to HVE, effective strategies for preventing radicalization must address the specific environment in which they are implemented. The challenges for City Heights, for example, are likely to be different from other at-risk communities across the country.

Looking to the *Prevent* strategy, it is clear one major error was a failure to engage stakeholders before implementation to determine the challenges unique to the area. What is more, the evaluation of *Prevent* occurred only *after* widespread criticism of the strategy's shortcomings. Ongoing community engagement would have not only better identified areas for program focus but would have also solicited ongoing feedback that could have been used to continually improve the strategy. This would have been the more effective approach, rather than waiting to review the strategy after several years of effort, funding and unfortunate community estrangement. Drawing on these lessons learned, it is possible to create a community-based program tailored to U.S. environments.

5.5 OBJECTIVES, SCOPE AND METHODOLOGY FOR A *MOSAIC OF ENGAGEMENT*

The threat of HVE will not dissipate independently. As well as law enforcement and intelligence work to stop individuals already plotting violent extremism, the United States can enhance its security posture by implementing strategies that work with communities to deter radicalization in the first place. This is the *Mosaic of Engagement.*

The program objective is to use a community-based strategy to improve the quality of life by reducing the risk of extremist recruitment, radicalization and related criminal activity. This goal is only feasible through engagement of *tipping point* stakeholders via Neighborhood Alliances, as well as community consensus that HVE reduction is the desired by-product of a safe community. Neighborhood Alliances depend on social networks representing a community-based hybrid of *Soft Power* and *Capillaries of Power* concepts.

Soft power is achieving a goal through attraction rather than coercion or payment.[16] Certainly, residents of any community want to enjoy the sense and experience of safety and security. When groups use relationships to collectively work toward an objective, policies that express certain values are more likely to be attractive when the values are shared. For example, Americans believe in volunteerism, as demonstrated in a 2012 Corporation for National and Community Service (CNCS) report.[17] More than 64 million Americans (a 5-year high) volunteered through a formal organization. The resulting dynamic is one of mobilizing cooperation, achieving desired outcomes without forcing groups to change their behavior.[18] Unfortunately, criminal elements (such as gangs, extremists and terrorist organizations) have realized that they can also use soft power as a means to garner support and new recruits.[19] The winner in the battles of soft power will be determined through self-organization. A community-driven effort is critical, as any suggestion of a "hard power," government-driven mandate may hinder willing stakeholder engagement, insomuch as they sense a lack of ownership in the process.

The process used to drive this soft power is best facilitated by a paradigm described by French philosopher and social theorist Michel Foucault, whose theories addressed the nature of power and the manner

---

[16]Nye, Jr., Joseph, S. (2004). *Soft Power, The Means to Success in World Politics.*
[17]Corporation for National and Community Service (12 December 2012). *Volunteering Among Americans Hits Five-Year High.*
[18]*Ibid.*, p. 15.
[19]Nye, Jr., Joseph, S. (2004). *Soft Power, The Means to Success in World Politics*, p. 25.

in which it functions.[20] Foucault's notion of *capillaries of power* is instructive with regard to the implementation of a community-based safety and security program. Governments typically engage in a hierarchical, top-down approach, whereas a capillary methodology assumes an individual is an active member who is not reduced to passive involvement because of their position in the organizational or community structure.

For Foucault, "power is not a hierarchical construct that is held by a dominant group and then wielded over the oppressed."[21] Rather, if society were a body, the power would circulate through the arteries and capillaries of society. The community capillaries of power are the individual stakeholders themselves who have chosen to organize, engage, identify, and prioritize challenges and develop solutions as demonstrated in City Heights. An example is a Neighborhood Alliance. Unfortunately, as with soft power, this capillaries of power concept has also been leveraged by extremist and terrorist organizations that understand the tactical advantages and recruitment potential of a self-organizing, decentralized group (e.g., terror cells) that agrees on a common objective—good or evil.

Drawing on the results of the *Prevent* strategy review, it is possible to develop a *Mosaic of Engagement* strategy in the United States. As described here, the *Mosaic* program consists of six critical phases, which although engaged linearly, actually function concurrently.

5.5.1 Phase 1: Scope

While there have been numerous advantages from the advent of the Internet, with regard to HVE, there have also been drawbacks. With social interaction increasingly occurring online, many people no longer know their next-door neighbors. This contributes to the potential for an HVE-enabling environment. The lack of personal residential relationships, coupled with the easy access to online organizations and ideologies, presents a formidable challenge to community-based efforts. Indeed, because one of the Internet's primary functions is to connect people and facilitate information sharing, the Bipartisan

[20]Kumar, K. (2009) *Foucault, Disciplinary Power, and the "Decentering" of Political Thought: A Marxian View.* http://people.su.se/~guarr/Ideologi/Kumar%20on%20Foucault%20Disciplinary%20Power%20and%20the%20Decentring%20of%20Political%2 (Retrieved: 27 June 2013).
[21]Frielick, S. (15 October 2005). *Capillaries of Power.* Enactivist: http://www.flexilearn.com/?p = 9 (Retrieved 27 April 2013).

Policy Center wrote "the use of the Internet to radicalize and recruit homegrown terrorists is the single-most important and dangerous innovation since the terrorist attacks of September 11, 2001."[22]

Whether radicalization and recruitment occurs online or within a community, implementing a *Mosaic* strategy requires ideas that counter the extremist ideology, as well as personal contact and face-to-face interaction via focus groups. This is where *tipping point* connectors are essential, particularly in immigrant communities. For instance, the examples of Adam Gadhan, Samir Khan and Tamerlan Tsarnaev disconnecting with their respective mosques before moving on to infamy suggests the religious leaders of those mosques were potential tipping point connectors. They challenged the extremist interpretations and protestations of the young men to the point where the latter were no longer welcome among the congregation.

While online capabilities can play an important part in implementing *Mosaic* (such as through online questionnaires, consultation and e-mail), focus groups give all participants the real-world, in-person relationships that are a critical part of the overall strategy. Removing the anonymous and impersonal interactions associated with online engagements is important. Face-to-face interactions facilitated by focus groups may reap the benefits of a collection of social and psychological activities borne of the forum itself. Important outcomes may yield increased personal participation; important nonverbal cues; personal commitment to the process; the ability to adapt the intended agenda to the needs of the group; and most importantly, the opportunity for the group to interact with each other.

The goal for these focus groups is to generate a range of ideas and perspectives, not necessarily to achieve consensus. The insights and experiences help define the community landscape and its challenges. Focus group engagement should be a dynamic process, reconvened on a predetermined timeline to maintain interest, information sharing and relationship building.

---

[22]Bipartisan Policy Center (2012). *Countering Online Radicalization in America.* National Security Program, Homeland Security Project.

5.5.2 Phase 2: Consensus

The identification of tipping point connectors is essential. By engaging the right people and helping them work together, communities can leverage their collective experience, energy and ideas. This process shifts the burden for detecting and deterring neighborhood safety and security issues onto those who have the capacity and moral responsibility to prevent them—the community. Success means striving for a safer community, which has a direct impact on reducing HVE. Individual and group behaviors to enhance and sustain a safe environment suggest these neighborhoods share a "community norm," strengthened by the bond of the basic human need for security. Although HVE is a subset of larger societal issues, families play an important role, particularly if they coalesce around the notion of a safe society. The literature demonstrates that family relationships can influence people to reconsider membership in terrorist or extremist organizations.[23]

This consensus phase employs the *soft power* approach, establishing Neighborhood Alliances with the expressed goal of creating and sustaining a safe community. This does not necessarily mean formally developing a new group or organization. Rather, communities can engage existing organizations that are involved with the "whole community," those that work at the nexus between community and government. These groups might include civil liberties and privacy organizations (ACLU); community safety organizations (Neighborhood Watch); fire services; social services; faith-based organizations; K–12 schools, as well as colleges and universities; health agencies and services; youth services and youth offender programs; probation and parole agencies; local businesses; and transportation services.

Each of these groups has a stake in identifying and prioritizing community challenges. To ensure the consensus building efforts are seen as legitimate and possible, great care must be taken to explain the process and its appropriateness to the task. If the process and outcomes are seen as predetermined, there is a great risk to process legitimacy. Lack of stakeholder engagement in the United Kingdom, exacerbated by an existing climate of fear, resulted in suspicions on the part of the Muslim community with regard to the implementation of

---

[23]Jacobson, M. (January 2010). *Terrorist Dropouts, Learning from Those Who Have Left.* The Washington Institute for Near East Policy, p. 31.

Prevent. Despite the program's stated goal of supporting "at-risk" communities, Muslims viewed the program as a solicitation to act as informants who provide intelligence on their own community, with everyone deemed suspect.

Consensus building is the process of arriving at unanimous agreement, allowing stakeholders to identify and collectively address cross-cutting issues or concerns. Consensus means all engaged parties are satisfied with the result because it has been designed to meet the needs of all interested stakeholders. In the case of community safety, a consensus might include sharing contact information to facilitate a neighborhood safety newsletter. It might also include designating "block captains" as representatives who communicate directly with law enforcement officers assigned to the area. As the saying goes, you can't please all of the people all of the time. Thus, in the spirit of democracy (and for the sake of reality), the goal of consensus building is to strive for support and agreement from most stakeholders. If an objective is achieved, it yields sustainable relationships that have the capacity to present a unified response to identifying and responding to community challenges.

5.5.3 Phase 3: Performance Measures

Although crime-related economic impact, recidivism and violent crime are critical issues, *Mosaic*'s success is to be measured by how communities coalesce around these issues; this as opposed to championing decreasing negative outcomes. The implementation criteria for performance measures must have a combination of quantitative metrics and finely granulated qualitative indicators. Examples include an increase in school enrollment by age and grade, rather than measurement of truancy rates; increases in employment for a specific age group, rather than incidence of gang-related arrests; or an increase in the number of participants in an after-school program, rather than non-arrest police contacts. Each of these measures provides Neighborhood Alliances with opportunities to share in the use of their resources for improving quality of life, which can be more valuable and inspirational than focusing on a reduction in the negative consequences of criminal activity. This differs from most traditional measurements of public safety programs. Crime statistics can offer some insight on progress, but neighborhood pride and sustained efforts are enhanced when this progress is identified and shared, consequently motivating the community to find other avenues for success.

The evaluation dimensions for this strategy are *cross-sectional,* *exploratory* and *interventional.* A cross-sectional evaluation offers a targeted view of a portion of the community, yielding a situational analysis of the program status. Public safety challenges are fluid, requiring real-time status information. Reviews of the past through a *retrospective* evaluation paired against a *prospective* idea of what the program hopes to yield are simply not timely enough to offer actionable, valuable insight. Exploratory dimensions search for answers or best practices, and interventional dimensions are used when the study is intended to change (or intervene on) something in the program or policy.

Although quantitative values can be definitive and instructive, it does not remove the need for other measurement instruments, such as surveys and citizen interviews. Analysis of this kind of feedback facilitates decisions and justification for program revision or adjustment. This is another component of the process where stakeholders maintain ownership of program measurement, analysis and modifications.

5.5.4 Phase 4: Community Engagement

Community engagement is designed on a theme of "taking care of each other." The success of a community-based program aimed at reducing crime generally (and the recruitment to extremist organizations specifically) is based on the level of community engagement. This is a valuable takeaway from the *Prevent* experience, inasmuch as the design of that program put itself at odds with the community it was intended to protect. As has been discussed, legitimizing ideologies and their narratives present an "us" and "them" perspective that separates groups from the broader community. This establishes a hostile relationship with government and society. Engaging focus groups helps determine the scope of the challenges and the people most at risk or impacted by those challenges. In City Heights, the citizens initiated the process as a result of the high crime rates and associated gang violence. Advertising the need for help, they were met by a police department seeking an opportunity, focused on the immediate challenge of drive-by shootings. Timing is everything. The groups came together, enlisting the assistance of the nonprofit organizations that were willing to fund the innovative initiative that became an impetus for an innovative movement.

Regardless of where *Mosaic* is implemented, it will be most effective if the details of the engagement are unique to the location. While some approaches will be similar across threatened areas, they must be tailored to the needs and makeup of the community where the strategy is put in action. For example, there are successes in City Heights as a result of the Safety Initiative that can be used to facilitate education and awareness of crime and extremism. Demographics suggest schools are the logical starting point.

The City Heights 2001−2010 stakeholder analysis shows one-third of the population was 17 years old or younger, with half of the population under the age of 30. What is not reflected in these numbers is the increasing presence of immigrants from Asia and Africa, specifically Pakistan and Somalia, nations that are experiencing significant security concerns. To reach the younger demographic and expose these age groups to the importance of a safe society, it made sense for City Heights to focus on schools as a place to focus their efforts. Going forward, this is also the logical environment where *Mosaic* may facilitate the risk reduction of future public safety challenges.

Inasmuch as City Heights has created a "School in the Park" in addition to "School-based Health Centers," the schools have also taken on an identity and feeling of a safe haven for members of the community. Parent Centers in the City Heights neighborhood emphasize the issue of family. The focus on and support for the family unit is a critical element in reducing the risk of HVE. As mentioned previously, every would-be terrorist has a family. Disjointed, unorganized communities create fertile ground for radicalization and recruitment. Conversely, communities that offer the capacity to unite and support families stand a better chance of disrupting or preventing susceptibility to the radicalization pathway in the first place. Like most urban street gangs, extremist groups attempt to become a "family," offering acceptance, appreciation and providing an opportunity for an individual to feel important. These groups fill the gap for alienated individuals living in unorganized and disconnected communities.

5.5.5 Phase 5: Information Sharing

Public safety issues for focus groups, consultation events and online questionnaires should be framed to obtain and share information on the following issues:

• Outlining the current status of crime and the identified risks.

- Briefing the community on the steps being taken to address those issues.
- Informing the community on how they can take part in crime reduction.
- Outlining where HVE is occurring (on the local, state, national and global levels).
- Explain which groups in the community are most vulnerable to being drawn into violent extremism and why.
- Explain which section(s) of the community are most likely to need support in resisting overtures from violent extremists.

As an example of why information sharing is critical, interviews with City Heights public safety personnel noted that property crime reporting was lower than the city average, suggesting unreported crimes.[24] This is common in immigrant communities, particularly when residents are living and working in the country illegally and therefore refrain from activities that could draw attention to their legal status. Additionally, immigrants who fled war-torn states often experienced brutal police tactics that are sometimes deadly. This can breed a culture of mistrust with police. For these reasons, the community may be more apt to live with crime rather than report it. By sharing information, however, it is possible to focus on previously unidentified threats to public safety, in turn enhancing the capacity to disrupt and prevent radicalization and recruitment.

Information sharing, however, is not only about identifying problems. It is also critical for distributing focus group findings, recommendations and improvements. Neighborhood Alliances can receive and disseminate information, such as the results of predetermined performance periods. Technology (social media networks and other online communication) can also be useful in sharing information about the ongoing activities and status of the performance evaluation.

5.5.6 Phase 6: Sustainability

Daily priorities, waning interest and the transient nature of many community residents make sustaining a public safety program challenging. The Price Charities partnered facilitators from San Diego State University with residents to enhance further evaluation efforts and to

---

[24]Interview with City Heights Security Director (15 August 2012).

begin the process of program sustainability. These volunteers not only completed the Safety Initiative Community Evaluations, but more importantly, trained residents to serve as evaluation facilitators themselves.

Some of the more critical elements of reducing the risk of crime and HVE are activities designed to counter rhetoric. The soft power and capillaries of power hybrid can serve a critical purpose at this juncture in the program implementation and evaluation. It is important to establish consistent messaging that makes full use of community resources, expertise and talent. Slogans that become part of the daily vernacular and are intergenerational can be invaluable (e.g., "Let's Take Care of Each Other" or "Making See Something, Say Something, Mean Something"), particularly if the community collectively creates their own motto. One way to achieve this kind of messaging is through a community website. City Heights developed such a site, which also included links to a variety of informational sources. Most important on the site are the entries touting community public safety successes.

Such a website and message, however, is rendered ineffective without community access to computers. Recognizing this, Price Charities donated 300 computers, along with requisite safety training, to the City Heights residents. This was a valuable investment in developing trust, independence and community responsibility. The Internet, however, can be a channel of extremist rhetoric and radicalization, and maintaining a community-led Internet safety effort is critical, particularly as it relates to protecting children from online exploitation and radicalization.

5.6 ONGOING CHALLENGES FOR RISK REDUCTION

The dynamic of HVE leaves much to be understood and researched. We know that it requires a foundational ideology, and that once embraced, it may progress along a radicalization trajectory toward violent action. Regardless of whether the enabling environment is physical or virtual, extremists do not live alone, and in their quest for answers and purpose, there may be opportunities for communities to reduce chances of a cognitive opening. As much as extremists seek communities, they also live in them. An extremist's contact (statements, behaviors, etc.) with other community members may offer an opportunity to disconnect from a legitimizing ideology.

Education and awareness on the issue of terrorism in the United States has been lacking, despite the extreme media focus on the threat from al Qaeda and the nation's homeland security efforts. Reactive in nature, the public rarely knows what threats the country faces and often only learns of such threats when law enforcement and counterterrorism professionals are responding to an incident. Opportunities to learn about, plan for and disrupt activities that are harmful to the community continue to be woefully insufficient. As equal partners, the community and the government can facilitate a system that may guard against irresponsible accusations of neighbors being engaged in suspicious activities. What is more, when a top-down government effort to prevent HVE focuses only on one community element (such as religion), the effort fails to address a community's basic need for public safety and potentially marginalizes the residents who are so critical for effective risk-reduction programs.

Lessons learned from the U.K.'s *Prevent* program, accompanied by successful public safety activities across the nation, such as in City Heights, provide opportunities for a *Mosaic of Engagement*. *Mosaic* acknowledges the diversity of extremist ideologies and is designed with necessary flexibility to respond to the different priorities of a community. The six stages of the process take great care and caution regarding a number of critical issues. It is as important to engage the community at the onset, developing metrics to determine outcomes, as it is to build trust. The most essential elements of such an effort depend on focusing on and responding to:

1. Cultural issues, as a result of the higher-risk population possibly consisting of an immigrant community.
2. Resistance from the dominant citizen population regarding the allocation of resources to support a program tasked to address a challenge seen as imported by the "at-risk" immigrant or target community.
3. Establishing the necessary stakeholder trust for the purpose of participating in surveys and focus groups.
4. Allowing the group to guide itself in a truly community-based and grassroots manner.

Although participation from the adult population is critical, every effort to introduce *Mosaic* into the school environment should be taken. This sets the stage for lifelong learning regarding safety and security, develops stronger familial bonds, and builds community pride. The chances of being perceived as a government intelligence-gathering program are removed if the community determines the activities, metrics and responses. The resulting group morality also yields important information regarding processes and activities deemed successful—program elements that could be replicated in future endeavors. Most important, these activities set the stage for additional academic disciplines to consider related research to enhance our understanding of HVE.

Mosaic is built on successes, not failures. Metrics emphasizing an increasing high school graduation rate (as opposed to the dropout percentage) or summer intern enrollment (in contrast to the juvenile arrest rate) builds community pride. There is nothing better than the feeling of being engaged in something special, particularly if it is for the greater good. The collective strength of a community and the resilience of a nation can resist and reduce the risk of HVE. Communities should unapologetically challenge everything violent extremists stand for. Understanding the threat is the first step for positive action.

FURTHER READING

Bipartisan Policy Center (2011). *Preventing Violent Radicalization in America*. National Security Preparedness Group, Washington, DC.

Bipartisan Policy Center (2012). *Countering Online Radicalization in America*. National Security Program, Homeland Security Project, Washington, DC.

Borum, Randy (2011). *Radicalization into violent extremism I: a review of social science theories*. Journal of Strategic Security, 4(4).

Brumfield, B. (23 February 2013). *Four Somalis in U.S. found guilty of supporting terrorists back home*. CNN U.S. http://www.cnn.com/2013/02/23/us/somalia-al-shabaab (Retrieved: 27 April 2013).

City Heights Safety Initiative website. http://www.safecityheights.org/about-us/our-history (Retrieved: 27 April 2013).

The City of San Diego, Redevelopment Agency, City Heights website. http://www.sandiego.gov/redevelopment-agency/cityhts.shtml (Retrieved: 26 April 2013).

Council on Foreign Relations (2011). *UK Counterterrorism Strategy, 2011*. http://www.cfr.org/counterterrorism/uk-counterterrorism-strategy-2011/p25325 (Retrieved: 10 February 2013).

Cragin, Kim (15 December 2009). *Understanding Terrorist Motivations. Testimony Presented Before the Committee on Homeland Security Subcommittee on Intelligence, Information Sharing and Terrorism Risk Assessment United States House of Representatives.* The RAND Corporation, Santa Monica, CA.

Dodd, V. (2009). *Government Anti-terrorism Strategy "Spies" on Innocent.* Guardian: http://www.guardian.co.uk/uk/2009/oct/16/anti-terrorism-strategy-spies-innocents (Retrieved: 25 February 2013).

Dutch General Intelligence and Security Service—AIVD (2005). Cited in Borum, Randy (2011).

Executive Office of the President of the United States. *Strategic Implementation Plan for Empowering Local Partners to Prevent Violent Extremism in The United States.* http://www.whitehouse.gov/sites/default/files/sip-final.pdf (Retrieved: 1 May 2013).

Farr, C. (19 January 2010). *Communities and Local Government Committee: Evidence.*

Frielick, S. (15 October 2006). *Capillaries of Power.* http://www.flexilearn.com/?p = 9 (Retrieved: 28 April 2013).

HM Government (2011). *Prevent Strategy: Equality Impact Assessment June 2011.* Crown, London, UK. https://www.gov.uk/government/uploads/system/uploads/attachment_data/file/97979/prevent-review-eia.pdf.

Ho, A.T. (2007). *Engaging Citizens in Measuring and Reporting Community Conditions: A Manager's Guide.* IBM Center for the Business of Government, Washington, DC.

Home Office website. *Prevent Strategy 2011.* http://www.homeoffice.gov.uk/publications/counter-terrorism/prevent/prevent-strategy/ (Retrieved: 16 February 2013).

Horgan, J. (2005). *Psychology of Terrorism.* Frank Cass Publisher, London, UK, 105–06.

Hunter, R. and Daniel H. (September 2011). *Perspective, Radicalization of Islamist Terrorists in the Western World.* FBI Law Enforcement Bulletin.

Information Sharing Environment website. http://www.ise.gov (Retrieved: 30 April 2013).

Johnston, K. (13 June 2011). *Prevent Strategy 2011: The Problem of Universities.* RUSI Analysis. http://www.rusi.org/analysis/commentary/ref:C4DF624BE8CCE8/#.URhZM45y5SUQ (Retrieved: 20 April 2013).

Kelling, G.L. and James Q.W. (March 1982). *Broken Windows.* The Atlantic. http://www.theatlantic.com/magazine/archive/1982/03/broken-windows/304465/ (Retrieved: 27 April 2013).

Kundani, A. (2007). *Spooked. Preventing Violent Extremism—Winning hearts and minds.* Department for Communities and Local Government, Preventing Violent Extremism Pathfinder Fund: Guidance Note for Government Offices and Local Authorities in England.

Lorenzo, V. (2010). *Countering Radicalization in America, Lessons from Europe.*

Martin, G. (2011). *Terrorism and Homeland Security.* SAGE Publications, Thousand Oaks, CA.

McCauley, C. and Sophia M. (Laurie Fenstermacher Ed., 2010), *Individual and Group Mechanisms of Radicalization, in Topical Strategic Multi-Layer Assessment (SMA), Multi-Agency and Air Force Research Laboratory, Multi-Disciplinary White Papers in Support of Counter-Terrorism and Counter-WMD.*

Nacos, B.L. (2007). *Al-Qaeda's propaganda advantage and how to counter it.* Perspectives on Terrorism, 1(4). http://www.terrorismanalysts.com/pt/index.php/pot/article/view/14/html (Retrieved: 22 April 2013).

National Counterterrorism Center (June 2012) *Radicalization Dynamics, A Primer.*

Nye, J.S., Jr. (2004). *Soft Power, the Means to Success in World Politics.* PublicAffairs™, New York, NY.

Omand, Sir David (2012). *The terrorist threat to the UK in the post-9/11 decade.* Journal of Terrorism Research, 3(1). http://ojs.st-andrews.ac.uk/index.php/jtr/article/view/412/371 (Retrieved: 22 April 2013).

Patel, F. (2011). RethinkingRadicalization. Brennan Center for Justice at New York University School of Law, New York, NY.

PET (October 2009). *Radikalisering og terror.* Center for Terroranalyse, Denmark.

Price Charities website: http://www.pricecharities.com/City-Heights-Initiative/ (Retrieved: 24 April 2013).

Richards, A. (2011). *The problem with "radicalization": the remit of "Prevent" and the need to refocus on terrorism in the UK.* International Affairs, 87(1).

Royal Canadian Mounted Police (June 2009). *Radicalization: A Guide for the Perplexed.*

Sageman, M. (2008). *Leaderless Jihad: Terror Networks in the Twenty-First Century.* University of Pennsylvania Press, Philadelphia, PA.

Susskind, McKearnan and Thomas-Larmer (1999). *The Consensus Building Handbook: A Comprehensive Guide to Reaching Agreement.* Sage Publications, Thousand Oaks, CA.

Task Force on Confronting the Ideology of Radical Extremism (March 2009). *Rewriting the Narrative: An Integrated Strategy for Counterradicalization.* Washington Institute for Near East Policy, Washington, DC.

Travis, Alan (20 August 2008). *MI5 report challenges views on terrorism in Britain.* The Guardian. http://www.theguardian.com/uk/2008/aug/20/uksecurity.terrorism1.

Wholey, J., Harry, H. and Kathryn, N. (Eds.), (2010). *Handbook of Practical Program Evaluation (3rd ed.).* Jossey-Bass, San Francisco, CA.

CONCLUSION

The Chinese warrior and philosopher Sun Tzu said, "If you know others and know yourself, you will not be imperiled in a hundred battles."[1] It is not sufficient to simply "know your enemy," as some have posited with regard to terrorism. With regards to HVE, the adversary and the target are one and the same. Addressing homegrown violence means we must look within our own society to identify threats and find ways to mitigate them.

Inasmuch as (regretfully) extremist ideologies are part of the fabric that makes up our diverse national tapestry, it is our reliance on democratic values that can help unravel the homegrown violence that threatens us. Programs designed to facilitate community and national coalescence on reducing the risk of HVE are enhanced by the very ideals we uphold as a democratic society. Securing a democracy is challenging, but there is a widespread and erroneous view that democracies are particularly vulnerable to terrorism and that we should curtail our rights and become something else in an effort to defend our nation. Recurrent recommendations for racial profiling suggesting, "Why can't we go through that model in order to narrow down who that perpetrator might be?"[2] would have been wasteful in the case of the Tsarnaev brothers, inasmuch a search for suspects of Middle Eastern descent would have removed them from a possible list.

To be sure, national security approaches must be balanced with our cherished rights of free practice of religion, free speech, right to privacy and all the freedoms that make the United States a great country. Yet, the fact is that no system of government (or absence of liberty) can guarantee complete security against violent extremists. What is more, no matter how effective our security policies and tactics, how advanced our technology and well-trained our law enforcement, future attacks will occur.

[1] Tzu, S. (1988). *The Art of War.* Translated by Thomas Cleary. Shambhala Publications, Inc.
[2] Jones, S. (22 April 2013). *Fox News Unwittingly Calls for Racial Profiling of Caucasians to Prevent Terrorism.*

To alter our government's view of liberty—indeed, to disrupt who we are as a nation—in response to the threat of HVE is to concede victory to the adversary. Terrorists seek a reaction and to reward their violence with a response that changes how we govern our citizens and residents grants power to the adversary. As this book has shown, the threat of HVE and the radicalization pathway are not limited to any one group or ideology. It is a crosscutting phenomenon that has the potential to impact all segments of our society. One cannot deny that Muslim Identity ideology played a major part in the terrorist threat of the last decade, but to focus the majority of our attention on that ideology, or worse still, to unfairly suspect a Muslim community of birthing violent extremists, is a woefully insufficient approach to the threat of twenty-first century violent extremism. More than that, in focusing on one group more than another, we begin to tread on the values of freedom and equality. In some cases, this kind of narrow focus on a specific community also betrays our proud history as a nation of immigrants.

Abandoning our principles at the first sign of adversity demonstrates to our adversary that we maintain a double standard—one for ourselves and one for "others," whoever that may be. Targeting entire communities for investigation based on erroneous stereotypes produces flawed intelligence, marginalizes the community that needs support, and emboldens opportunities for extremists to recruit. The simple truth is there is no terrorist profile, and we do a grave injustice to our national security efforts and our country if we act as if there were.

Our security programs must be based on evidence and facts. The evolution of counterterrorism into an evidence-based discipline will engender public support and credibility. Understanding the people, processes and outcomes associated with HVE recruitment, radicalization, and violent action arms communities with important knowledge. Messaging—real or virtual—is the strongest weapon our adversaries possess, but words and ideas can be overcome. They can also be identified and countered. Terrorists do not operate in a vacuum. Every homegrown violent extremist has a family, one that can either facilitate radicalization by inaction or halt it through knowledge and public and community support. Shared information regarding the groups, their ideologies and their objectives goes a long way toward creating an environment that is more resistant to HVE.

Communities do not need a government to dictate their shared values and principles. Who we are as a country is not bestowed on us; it grows out of our population. Yet, all communities can benefit from guidance on best practices, effective services and accurate knowledge that can enhance safety (and by consequence, reduce opportunities for grievances to mature into violence). A holistic community approach enhances public safety, and it addresses the threat of HVE in a way that can prevent terrorism and not just stop terrorists. We have a tremendous interdisciplinary capacity, using a plethora of tools, technology and personal conversations, to educate and assist communities with efforts to improve their quality of life.

While many of the ideas and concepts presented in this book are important for addressing the growing threat of HVE, more work remains. The United States needs academics and professionals from all disciplines to take a more focused, nuanced look at violent extremism and continue to study and understand how ideology and grievances breed the potential for violence and terrorism. We must better understand how individuals traverse the radicalization pathway and develop more approaches for helping disrupt that dangerous evolution. Much like the community focus described in the *Mosaic of Engagement* strategy, it will take all professionals and scholars working in concert to continue pushing us toward a greater understanding of HVE and the most effective ways to address and prevent it.